Miracules̈

© Copyright Sheri Hauser 2008, 2020, 2026
Published by Glorybound Publishing, Camp Verde, AZ
SAN 256-4564
4th Ed
Printed in the United States of America
ISBN 1-60789-254-5   978-1-60789-254-0
Library of Congress Cataloging-in-Publication data is available on file.
Hauser, Sheri, 1957-

       Miracules̈/Sheri Hauser
       Includes biographical reference.

  1. Ancient Mysteries.   2. Mindfulness and Meditation.

  I. Title

www.gloryboundpublishing.com
www.sherihauser.com

Miraculeś
Mirror of God

The Spiritual Connection.
A discourse and meditation of five holy books. The rainbow of
God in the seven spirits from Isaiah 11

by Sheri Hauser

Glorybound Publishing
Camp Verde, AZ
in the year 2026

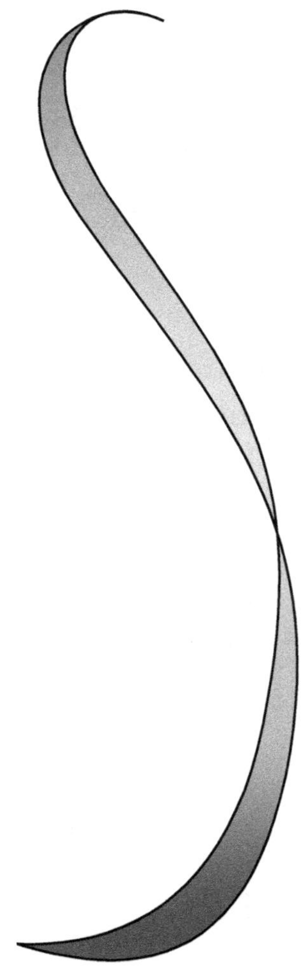

Dream Cachë

Welcome to Sheri's dream cache releasing what has been kept hidden until now. There are
stores of riches kept in a vault up to this day, which open the door of understanding the
voice of God in dreams as answers to prayer. The wind, the storm, the rain and the
lightening of God is coming. Feel the wind? There is always a gentle breeze just
before the tornado. Oh how we have looked for the eye of the storm in this
world in which we live, yet we have not found it. We have prayed, yet we
are not healed. We have spent countless hours on our knees without
finding our deliverance. Our children remain on drugs; our families
are still in bondage; we are yet poor and destitute. Our Churches are
poor, filled with empty pews and singers off cue. Where are the answers
to our prayers? We have been tricked by our enemies. They have snuck in and
left seeds of doubt which grew into a cancer eating away at our faith in God. Our vision
has been clouded by our own
sinfulness and lust for the things of this world. Yet we continue to seek for a force outside
ourselves which will save us from this dreadful condition which we are in. Where is He?
Take encouragement, friends, I have brought a fresh shipment of hope: It's the hope of
hearing the voice of God for yourself. Just like Moses heard the voice of the Lord and
brought salvation to the children of Israel, He is bringing the same today. Has God
changed? No. Suppose you ask a question in prayer: Do you expect an answer?
There is one, you know? I am here to help you reach out to God in a special way
and enable the enemies of doubt within your life to be crushed and conquered.
What I bring is a bridge to faith. We attempt to reach a God we do not
know; only have heard about from those going on before us. But, when
we reach into that darkness, we are unsure of a connection: Will there
be a hand reaching back to us? We don't really know. That is faith,
my friend. Faith reaches into the unknown seeking something you
are unsure of while trusting that there will be an answer on the
other side. Welcome to my dream Cachë. It is like a jewelry
box filled with gems, sparkling in the moonlight: dreams
that come to life as the voice of God dances through my
head night after night. And, He wants the same for
you. He told me, so. Your dreams and visions
can be a bridge to a relationship with God
giving encouragement, hope, help, and
direction hidden in this vault of
wondrous pictures
sent straight
from
heaven.
I have propped open
for you five doors
and a window .
I encourage
you to
learn to seek God through learning to understand His voice as it
comes to you His way, now as you are comfortable accepting it. Remember,
God came in thunder, storm and a wind in times before. Why wouldn't He now? May
I present this shipment of Grace. For it is by the Grace of God that we are saved. Remember that.

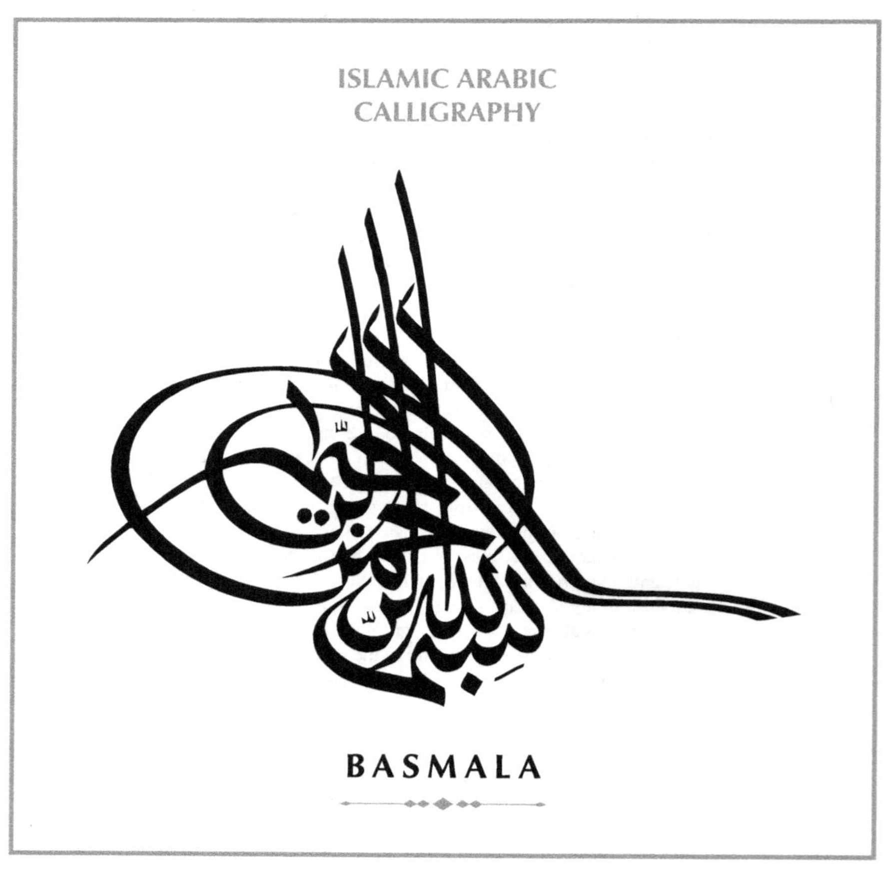

An Arabic verse of Basmala "In the name of Allah, the Entirely Merciful, the Especially Merciful" in Arabic Callighraphy

Holy Books Referenced in the Text

Certainly there are many more holy books which could be included in the dissertation, but I limited it to these:

Christian New Testament (Christian) New International Study Bible is the work of a transdenominational team of Bible Scholars. It was made by over a hundred scholars working directly from the best available Hebrew, Aramaic, and Greek texts. It had its beginning in 1965 by committee from the Christian Reformed Church and the National Association of Evangelicals. Names of translators and editors may be secured from the International Bible Society, translation sponsors of the New International Version. 1820 Jet Stream Drive, Colorado Springs, CO 80921 U.S.A. Published by Zondervan, Grand Rapids, Michigan 49530.

Holy Catholic Bible (Catholic)

New American Bible translated from the original languages with critical use of all the ancient sources including the revised Psalms, and the revised New Testament. Authorized by the board of Trustees of the Cofraternity of Christian Doctrine and approved by the Administrative committee/board of the National Conference of Catholic Bishops and United States Catholic Conference. Included are the books: The Pentateuch, The Historical Books, the Wisdom Books, the Prophetic Books, the Gospels, the New Testament Letters, and the Catholic Letters. Oxford University Press, Oxford New York.

Qur'aan (Islam)

Notes from the translation of the Qur'aan translated by Abdullah Yusuf Ali 1998. Published by Islamic Educational Services 2648 RT 206, M.T. Holly N.J. 08060

Tanakh (Jewish)

The Holy Scriptures, produced by the Jewish Publication Society, made directly from the traditional Hebrew text into the idiom of modern English. It represents the collaboration of academic scholars with rabbis from the three largest branches of organized Jewish religious life in American. Jewish Publication Society September 15th, 1985. {Hebrew-English Tanakh. Jewish Publication Society. Philadelphia, 2003}

The Book of Mormon (Latter Day Saints)

An account written by the hand of Mormon upon plates taken from the plates of Nephi. Included are the plates of Nephi, Plates of Mormon, Plates of Ether, and the plates of Brass. Translated by Joseph Smith, Jun. Published by The Church of Jesus Christ of Latter-day Saints Salt Lake City, Utah, U.S.A.

Why Write a Book Like This?

Miracules took a long time to write because of the research and commitment involved in the process. At first I began to understand an interpretation of the seven spirits of God — *presence, wisdom, understanding, counsel, might, knowledge, and the fear of the Lord*— mentioned in Isaiah 11:

> A shoot will come up from the stump of Jesse;
>> from his roots a Branch will bear fruit.
> 2 The Spirit of the Lord will rest on him—
>> the Spirit of wisdom and of understanding,
>> the Spirit of counsel and of might,
>> the Spirit of the knowledge and fear of the Lord—
> 3 and he will delight in the fear of the Lord.

My goal is not to convert individuals to a religion, but to open up understanding of how to hear God's voice for ourselves within whatever orientation we come from. God is big and can talk however and to whomever He desires; why would it be preposterous to assume He has not spoken through time to many? Therefore I have included insertions from several holy books to make my case that He *just might be* the same God.

Think of it like this: Each of us has been given a piece of paper *symbolic of our ideas concerning who God is*. None of us has a whole piece of paper because there is no way we could totally understand Him. So, each of us is missing parts of the paper—some more than others. How would I know which piece of your paper is missing and how would you know which piece of mine is not there? Seems like the most reasonable solution is to ask the one who gives the paper and the pencils to help understand who He is.

I would be remiss to assume the reader questions my understanding of the holy books, so I will define the history of learning. It was impossible to study the holy books apart from their religion, so I did an extensive dive into each.

Catholicism was easiest for me because I was born into the religion and received my first communion at age five. It is based on what is considered the Old Testament and the New Testament. Both are included in this book. My mother, Gayle, showed me the true spirit of

Catholicism helping me to recognize it is not about attending services and memorizing prayers, but honoring God by valuing others.

I confess that I did not go much further than my first holy communion in the Catholic religion because my mother was ex-communicated when she divorced my father. Consequently, I was not very impressed with the faith because it had too many rules with domineering priests.

However, they teach honor to God and excel in reverence. My husband, Paul, went further in the faith continuing to become an altar boy. He says it was a valuable experience in helping to instill clear ethical principles of living.

When I graduated from high school and converted to mainstream Christian, I attended Bible College for a year. It was a compressed study of the entire Bible that provided a good foundation for my faith.

Endorsements with Thanksgiving

I began studying the Book of Mormon and a young professional pilot and elder of the Church Latter Day Saints, Scotty, explained many of the details of their faith. He was living with us at the time, so we spent countless hours delving into the religion. He permitted me to accompany him to a couple of services—with the understanding that I was doing research for a book and not intending to become converted. As I spoke with him and read the Book of Mormon (and the Pearl of Great Price) I truly came to see the dedication of these early individuals who believed in what they felt to be true. When I completed my study with Scotty, he presented me with a painting of Moroni. I hung it on the wall in my office for a long time. The picture is in the front of the Book of Mormon. It depicts a man kneeling at the base of a tree with some golden tablets. He is muscular and visibly moved. You can see on his face that he realizes that if he believes they are from God, then he will need to make a costly choice in his life. It has a message we all should adhere to. Thank you to Scotty for being willing to share some of the gems of his belief.

Cardiovascular Surgeon, Dr. Bashir Chowdry shared with me the best resources to understand the Qur'aan and the Muslim faith. As he followed my journey and saw I joined in the Ramadan fast, he invited my husband and I to the closing ceremony at the Mosque. I joined with the women on their side while Paul stayed with Dr. Chowdry. During this time in my life, I was working as an ICU nurse and cared for many of his patients after they had heart surgery. He commented to me once, "Sheri, what do you do differently from the other nurses? I send my patients to recover under your care and none of them seem to have complications. What is it that you do?"

I replied, "Oh, Dr. Chowdry, that is an easy question. I pray for them."

He raised his eyebrows and exclaimed, "That is awesome. Keep doing it because surely, there is power in those prayers."

I really appreciated Dr. Chowdry's willingness to share the religious ceremonies with me, even though he realized I was not going to convert. He trusted my motivation. He even permitted me to pray with the women at his home in a designated prayer room to cap off the following year's Ramadan. It was an honor.

Dr. Quazi, Nephrologist, was one who shared regular messages at the Mosque. He took a trip to the holy place [when his son turned of age] and brought back some water from the well. I was delighted when he shared it with me. And, when his son recited the Qur'aan at his ceremony, Dr. Quazi invited my husband and I to attend. It was in a neighborhood near to our house. We were happy to join in his celebration for his son. This is a special time in their life.

I truly appreciate Medical Director and Pulmonoligist, Dr. Nawaz Qureshi for joining arm in arm in our search for truth. One of the first dreams at the start of the entire search included him. The dream told me that he was searching for the same thing I was—to understand what it means to know God; not about Him, but Him personally. I had not met the Dr. as he was in a prominent position in the hospital and was very cautious to speak with him. I waited for an opportune time and, when I was in an elevator with him, I told him the dream. His response surprised me, "I didn't know this was what I am looking for. When you find it, please come back to me and let me know. For surely I am intrigued at this dream."

So, I did return to him...again and again. He was happy to listen and read the writings that I jotted down at that time. We became good friends. When his wife died, he asked me to accompany him at the grave site. And, as I released the first editions of the dream books, he was delighted to put them on his shelf.

All of the men above added their signature to my first copy of this book when it was printed. This is an honor because it proved to me I fulfilled the mission of showing respect and honor to their holy book and faith without causing them to feel pressured to convert.

It occurred to me, "What if all of these are seeking the same God I am, but He is simply showing Himself as a God of a different color?"

Isn't He in and through everything because His hand created all of it?

We are dull to assume their view of the creator is invalid because it is not ours. We condemn books and faiths which we know nothing about. Our ignorance is expanded by the lack of willingness to try. The difference with me is that I read these books. I studied them as intensively as the one I had been given since childhood. And, I came to respect the words, their intent and the amazing depth of spiritual messages.

This is not a dissertation on religious tolerance but a shaking to wake up and be willing to look outside of the four walls you were raised within to see there is a bigger God out there than the One you have come to know. And, if you are willing, then your life will become more rich by the expansion of your spirit.

I admit that I don't agree with all of what each holy book says—in fact I can't agree with any of them totally. But, I think of it like walking on the beach picking up pebbles and shells. I can't possibly put all of them in my pocket anyway, so I may as well select the ones I like and leave the rest for others.

It wasn't my idea. Originally, after I received the baptism of the Holy Spirit in 2001, I began having vivid dreams and visions. After some time I figured out how to interpret them. The amazing thing I recognized was they were answers to my questions—some voiced and others silent prayers—and if I took the time to figure out the mystery of the dream then the answer became evident. I was perfectly happy asking questions and receiving answers from the universe. It was my secret passageway to heaven. But then this happened—

Why I Write

And when they ask you why you did it, what will you say?

I'll tell them the truth.

And, what is that, Sheri?

I became friends with someone who has no hands. He has arms, but he is without hands. I'm not sure how that happened, but it is not mine to question God.

And, what happened is that my ability met his need. For, I had hands and was willing to do things he couldn't do.

I didn't even notice, at first. He was such a dear sweet companion and never asked anything of me. I never noticed that he was impaired in this area. It seemed like his personality made up for it. Certainly, it did not affect his ability to reach out to my heart day after day.

And, I found myself desiring to get to know him in a closer way. He was the most interesting person, always full of encouragement for me. He always had some words of wisdom and insight into life to offer me. And, I would take those words back with me and share them with others. They found them to be profound and thought I was very smart. Short talks became lingering siestas and we lounged side by side, often, on the couch, at the park, in the car. We could talk about everything and anything. I shared my heart with my special friend.

Then in anticipation of Valentine's Day, I wanted to give him a valentine. He knew that I was already very emotionally attached, so I didn't want to give him something mundane; I wanted it to be special. So, I wondered, "What could I give Him?"

Then, it dawned on me—I could give him the use of my hands whenever he needed them. He was so humble and didn't ask for things, that I had never heard him ask before. Certainly, He had things that he wanted done. I could see that all of his needs were being met, but what about his wants. That is what a holiday is for—to give someone something that he doesn't ask for, but wants. It's a trick that those who care for one another play on each other. They attempt to demonstrate their love in secret ways. It's fun to figure out what someone secretly wants, and then have it ready to give at the appointed special time. It causes hearts to soar when their desires are fulfilled by someone that they know has pure motives—just to show their love.

And, I realized that there were probably things that he would do, if someone was willing to linger when he asked. You know? When someone asks you what you want for Christmas, then pauses to let you respond, it gives you a chance to think, then respond. I thought, "What if I did this with my friend?"

So, I did. On Valentine's Day, I gave my special one a note from my heart. I gave him a pass to do whatever he wanted to with my hands. And, I reserved the pass for his desires, not his needs. I wanted it to be a special day.

I remember it so clearly—I put on my best smile and with tenseness in the air, I delivered my gift, that Valentine's Day. I presented him with my hands. I think he had heard it before, because his face didn't move, at first. I could almost feel his heart sink—because all of a sudden I realized how important the words were to him. Apparently, others had told him this, but then turned too quickly, not waiting for his response. I could tell. Like someone in a wheel chair denied access, once more—he puts up a shield to protect his heart from disappointment *one more time*.

But, I was serious. And, he came to realize it when I held out my hands, then didn't turn around.

He taunted me because his heart had been broken so many times. He said, "Are you sure? You have no idea what I want."

And, I didn't. But it didn't matter to me. I had used these hands for 40 years selfishly, without even thinking of my friend who had none. And, now that I came to know him in a special way, I would gladly help. Because, I knew he wouldn't cut them off from my body, he only wanted some help with the things in between my needs.

So, I kept waiting for his response. I waited three months, every day returning to the same table at the cafe to have coffee with him. Each day we met and I didn't pester him. I could tell that he was thinking. It was very important to him. I had no idea how important it was when I offered. It seemed like a small thing to me.

Then, one morning, very early, he woke me because he had decided what to do with his *pass*. He brought me to his house and opened a closet stuffed with unopened envelopes. He said, "These are the letters for my children, yet unopened."

And, I said, "Who wrote these letters?"

He responded, "Sheri, I wrote many and my friends wrote back. But the letters are stuck in the span where they are caught in between. I have no one who will send them out. They are like *my voice coming to them*. Each one is specially marked with a date and time. Each response carefully planned before time. All written by my wisdom. Without a mailman, how will they ever be delivered?"

And, I picked up a letter, only to notice my name was on the top of the stack. As my face lit up, he nodded in confirmation that I could open it.

He planned a Valentine's gift for me, as well. He was just waiting for me to come to pick it up. As I scanned the words, I could barely see the words through the tears of joy. It was his response to my plea written several years ago requesting to come to his prayer closet…and now I was here.

So, I asked him, "What do you want me to do with the letters?"

He replied, "Mail them at just the right season."

I go to his house often, now and, he hands me a fresh stack of letters. It is amazing how he combined the answer to my letter with the desire I had to give a gift to him. I became a mailman that day. It is just a little job for someone that I found to be very special.

Battle of Nun

On the same day at the Battle of Nun, there came together nation against nation, world against world. "Kingdoms at arms," they called it; for there had never been a battle such as this and there would never be again.

With a mighty show of strength those who had been pushed back locked arms in a line. Their numbers dwindled by the tenacity of the battle over such a long time. Wild animals had consumed many in the Forest of Have Not. What they needed never came and they found themselves lost and alone in the overgrown prickly underbrush. Consumed by oppression and torn by despair they curled up into a ball and felt the light slide from their eyes. Taunted daily by the beasts which freely roam within the Have Not Forest. The enemy taunts the wants; pounds a nail in the flesh and drives it on in with a crooked branch from a pinning heart of the Forest of Have Not.

On this day at the Battle of Nun there came together a people of one purpose, united in value. Those with clear eyes pure desire and no remorse; the few who clung to the vision of winning. They had lost their guns and ammo long ago having traveled far across uneven territory and muddy canals. The weight of the man made weapons having grown heavier with each step until one by one their rifles and bullets were flung aside to rust in the Forest of Have Not. And, the forest let out a wicked laugh for it had gained and they had not. Surely, they had thrown away their last hope. Who could win without a weapon?

But, these soldiers trekked along through muddy waters with wet boots more worried about their ability to press on than what they had thrown aside. Convergence of tenacity and wonder of energy they banned together and moved on through the Forest of Have Not.

Then came the day of the Battle of Nun a confirmation of eternal significance. For, when the few gathered arms and overlapped elbows they gained strength from one another.

A brave one took the lead, grasp a bleeding hand and pressed forward through the thicket. Day after day they placed one foot in front of the other seeking their deliverance and looking toward salvation.

All at once the leader gave a call, "I see it: Come follow me!" And, the rest tagged along.

What man of fortitude and bravery unsurpassed to take the lead at such a time as this. For, indeed he was the furthest into the Forest of Have Not refusing to look back, yet clinging to those who needed hope and help to get out.

Wild animals howling in the proximity and thunder clouds crashing overhead, they ducked and dashed amidst the tall trees. Shielded in the shadows of the almighty, they passed through with agility.

In the few final steps each one recognized that there was a reason he had tossed aside his weapons because there was no way to hold the very thing he assumed would protect him and to hold the hand of another. Their arms had become the arms of someone else.

With a shout the leader lifted his arm holding his red feathered cap high for all to see, "We're here!"

They had reached the Field of Abundance. On the edge of the field, each paused for a solemn moment gazing back at the place now become history: the Forest of Have Not. The Field of Abundance open before them was an amazing sight, yet the trauma of the run continued to hold them in a frigid state. Memories of fatigue, hunger and hateful eyes of oppression had burned deep within their soul, paying their toll. And, there was recognition within each of these ragged soldiers that he needed to make a clear choice to face the Forest of Have Not or to face the Field of Abundance; to cling to the pain or embrace the change.

Within the pregnant pause two soldiers let go of arms and fled in fear returning to the Forest of Have Not. Grown accustomed to being without, they were not prepared to be in a state of with. This is the Land of Have; the place where you never thought possible, is; the culmination of the dream; the door of the answer to the question: The birth of the expectancy.

And, in that day at the Battle of Nun, the enemy lost 100 to 1 because the soldiers found that just beyond the ridge a mighty army was waiting and prepared. So as they continued their footed flight just rounding the corn patch with enemies on their heels a little behind, a new army came from behind the ridge. They had waited for such a time as this. They wedged themselves in between the Soldiers and their enemies slaughtering the to the last one.

The soldiers stopped running and kissed the ground and hugged one another in amazement. In accordance to the decree of the King, each one was given a portion of the land according to his acts of bravery during his time in the Forest of Have Not. In addition, the King gave the army to protect them from their enemies.

Now the soldiers don't need to run and they don't need to fight. They need not fear the enemies of the Forest of Have Not because they live safely in the land of Have in the Valley of Abundance. The Forest of Have Not is always nearby, but they can choose to avoid it by staying in their Land of Have being protected by the Army of the King.

But, what of the two soldiers who returned to the Forest for fear?

Oh, out of love two brave soldiers took the army with them and returned to the Forest of Have Not on special mission. Secretly at night they slithered into the darkness on their bellies and found the lost ones forlorn, torn and moaning in the distance. No enemies were near because they assumed the battle was won over these two. They heard the echoes of the spirit moaning as the two cried in the wilderness. And the enemies reasoned that as long as they heard the cries, they knew they didn't need to pursue them because they were bound by their own grief.

But, when the two brave soldiers came with their army, they too followed the moans of the spirit to the forlorn ones. They were not afraid because they recognized the moans of the sad soul lost in the Forest of Have Not; they were echoes of their own soul in a time they had known before.

Rapid as a flint to light they tossed their friends over their shoulders and carried them out. Boldness and strength unmatched guarded by those given to protect they carried their friends out of the forlorn situation before their enemies realized the moaning had ceased.

When the enemies recognized the moans were no more, they ran to the place they had stashed their foes in the Forest of Have Not and were met with their own vision of Have Not. In anger they blamed one another for their lack of attentiveness. But, who would have suspected that those freed would come back to the place they had been bound to free their friends? Enemies never free one another, so the thought was never on their mind in the Forest of Have Not.

There was a whirlwind of anger and agitation in the Forest of Have Not and a spark caught wind to become a raging fire which quickly engulfed the entire region.

And, there was nobody sent to put out the fire. None was sent to rescue those engulfed in the flames. Why would anyone want to put out a fire which was to destroy a forest of want? Let the fire consume the Forest of Have Not.

So, it burns to this day.

Threads of Mercy

Threads of mercy, threads of light
threaded through my spirit tonight.
Stitched and sewn, enlightened and shown
threaded through my spirit tonight.
Threads of purpose bind my soul.

Mesmerizing colors embedded within
inside my being coincide to begin
to thread His mercy and spin His light.
Effervescent echoes, deep insight.

Threads of mercy may I true be to you
Indeed, in love, in might through and through.

A weaving holiness, unity with above,
then,
returned all at once
just like before
threads of mercy opens the door.

O Mercy Calls

God of mercy, come to us.
Of mercy we call on the name.

God of glory look our way
O mercy call our name.

Savior of comfort, joy and delight
Reign bright. Become might.
Turn what would be into what is.
Make what cannot not stand; understood.

O God of mercy, fill the place
Bring wonder, love and grace

O God of mercy, lean Your ear
Look our way. Do come near.

O mercy calls my name.
For you have called me back.
It's mercy just the same
Love without lack.
Mercy to me, mercy to you.
Mercy to those who never knew.

O mercy calls your name
May it never be the same.

The Island of Runaground

Battered by the storms of life, she sought refuge under a log that had drifted ashore. The boat had gone down under the intense pounding of the waves against the hull of her hard head. She was going to do it 'her way'. And, so it was. She did. Without listening to others, she sculpted her future, her figure and her career. Beautiful, yet not adored; Adorned yet untrue set on a mission of success built from mental strain and determination, she pushed the mentally fragile ones aside, refusing to allow their intrusion into her thoughts. With steel eyes and a hardened heart, she pushed aside emotion laughing at reproach. She was right; her life proved it was so. Setting sail alone; this fair weather queen adorned her own bow for there was no need for another. Everyone knows that a craft has but one bow needing to be adorned. She did it herself. She sailed up and down the coast keeping close in to shore to be sure to be noticed her time was all taken.

"Surely," she reasoned, "A tight schedule proves ones worth; therefore, I am valuable."
So, she sailed. Back and forth year after year up and down the coastal waters rightly adorning her craft with herself. At first there were onlookers, gazing from ashore. Novelty demands attention. But, soon they were called to their own purpose and turned from hers. Ah, she stacked up fleeting moments one upon another; pressed into short relationships without depth. Together they almost mounted to something; yet in the rain of time they melted.

Without an audience, who would dance? Without onlookers, why adorn yourself? If no one cares, why take the boat out at all? So she tied it to the dock in the fall and paid a mooring fee. For, who knows, perhaps she will be sailing again next season? There is a cost to being tied to a stable relationship. And, for a while, she paid it.

But, when spring came and the flowers began to bloom, there was hope in the air. She went to the dock and visited her vessel. She buffed and waxed; contemplated and mulled ideas; to stay tied for another year or launch out once more. Surely there was some new audience that needed to recognize the beauty of her stature. Amidst fair weather, she set a course due East; fixing her gaze upon the horizon she sailed into unknown waters. Without a compass, she followed her reason.

Without compassion for those she left behind, sailing away was easy. A hard heart can know no other because in order for a heart to connect to someone else it must be softened to have the strands intertwined with the other one. Hers was as a stone; she was used to tossing it into the boat whenever she desired; and sailing off into the wind of her whim.

She ran aground at midnight at 'who knows where.' How could she know? There was no compass and the lights had gone out long ago. Recognizing she was in a perilous position having the boat torn from asunder, she prepared to drown. Saying her prayers, and taking a final gasp of the night air, she jumped overboard. Her body prepared for the worst, she was surprised that the water was not cold, but warm. With plenty of air in her lungs it was a natural inclination to push off the bottom when her toes reached it with their extension. And, the push was just enough to bring her to the surface. Aha, what do you know? The shore was right there. Why would she opt to drown when she could swim ashore? Pride, remorse and refusal to face what she had turned her back on? Were they reasons enough to die? It was her choice; and, who would know? She could make it seem as though it was not her fault; being a victim of circumstances. After all, she was aground on a rock. The caption could read, "She went down between a rock and a hard place."

Yet, she went ashore and hid from herself on an island in the middle of nowhere alone amidst the storm and buried her face in remorse hating herself for being who she was. The devil taunted her in the unmet dreams of her desire until the sun came up.

Hearing a noise, she squinted her eyes to see a vision appearing in some distance and growing ever near. As much as she tried to hide her eyes; who can hide from a vision? The man with deep wrinkles in his face came right up to her and held out his hand. Without a word, she took it. He had no request from her. She could be anyone she wanted with him. So, she left her past behind and went fishing. Sure, the wreckage was in the distance, but neither of them mentioned it.

And, the wreckage has become a breeding ground for new fish. So, the old man and the lost sailor dine and share with others on the Island of Runaground around the fires of delight in a place where the only expectation that they have from one another is being who they really are.

Bottled for a Time

I put in on the north shore and drifted with the west wind
A kid came by and checked me out
I put in at the beach again and rolled with the waves
A surfer paused then sailed on by.
But she returned to see me, and we said, "Hi."
I put in again amidst tall waves and floated for miles rising and
lowering with each crest of the wave.
I rounded the bend on time to be picked up by the ferry crew.
They looked me over and kept on going leaving me adrift
amidst and fully intact.
Then my time finally came and I washed up to shore.
The tide went out and I was no more.
Time in a bottle had come to me with no retreat
Its due.

Keeper of the Pocket Watch

Time has a debt, you know?
Come payment due
Time has a debt, you know?
When it has to come through?
For, if He is in charge, then it must do as He says
Fulfilling its obligation rising from its bed.
It cannot stall when He comes to call.
He's in charge of it all.
"He's the keeper of the pocket watch," I have been told.
With His eyes upon time, watching it unfold

Time has a debt, you know?
Come payment due.
Time has a debt, you know
when it has to come through?
Mistress of the moment, wisdom turns the key
Balancing accounts for all to see.
Time has come and time was due
Hour by hour increments flew
Mechanics of life amidst strife
Risen to find, needing a rewind

O keeper of the pocket watch come wind some more today.
Keeper of the pocket watch make time obey.

Eat the Cheerios or the Box

This book is for you who know there is a wall between you and God; and realize there is a wall between where you are and where you want to be. Because, perhaps, after looking over all the book titles, you feel overwhelmed because you are still on the other side of the wall. And, like a college student looking to receive a degree in a few years, you feel you can't wait that long to graduate. You have a burning in your chest that won't let you rest.

Your soul is starving. And, you have been so long without food that you have looked for other things to eat. But, what they have fed you is the cardboard box instead of the Cheerios. And, you look at them chewing on their own cardboard with plastic smiles on their faces and wonder, "Certainly they know. For, they are filled, but not satisfied."

And, if you find that you are surrounded with good things. If you have a nice family, decent job and comfortable living conditions, yet are miserable; this book is for you.

But, before I pour Cheerios into your bowl, let's see if you're ready. Maybe you're not. Here are a few questions to test your soul. Your soul is like a roast cooking in a pot. It starts out tough as can be, then, becomes tender. It doesn't start out being tender. We are all at different degrees of tenderness in our relationship with God. Many times we need to get back into the pot and simmer some more before we are ready to be served and serve others. The tenderness of your soul is not anyone else's responsibility; and they can't do it anyway. It is yours.

We would like to think that it is God's responsibility to make our soul tender to Him and others. Sometimes, like a pot roast, we assume that *over time* we will become tender. That's not true: If the cut of meat is bad, time won't change it. If our soul is *bad* time only preserves it for later.

Oh, and we think, "Add some seasonings and certainly this roast will become tender."

So, we add. We add religious meetings, scripture study, memorization, and discipline. We add things to help tenderize our soul. And, we reason, that over time, through *seasons* of study and discipline, we will become tender to God.

But, this doesn't work. So, we leave conventional religion and go seeking. Still we are looking for the Cheerios that we know are in that box—It says so in the cover. We believed we were looking for the *presence of God* and, certainly, *God is not in religion,* so we jump from one pot to the next. Sometimes we choose a bigger pot, and sometimes a smaller one—bigger group of followers. But a pot is a pot and we are bound by external elements which are out of our control.

What I have found is that we each have a garden which our soul is grown in. Oh what wonderful plants, rockeries and statues are in that garden! It is a wonderful place. But, we don't know how to sit and enjoy the garden because we keep looking over the fence at the neighbor's.

We need to learn to be content in our own garden. We need to pull our own weeds and tend our bushes when they get out of control.

Yet, there will continue to be unrest in your soul until you learn to leave the gate open. You see, my friend, of all the messages I have to share this is the most profound: God has a garden, too. And, He isn't waiting for us to come to His garden, but for us to leave the gate open so He can come to ours.

Oh, we are worried, "What if He comes when the roses are not blooming? What if He comes when I am in the middle of weeding and finds me in my work clothes?"

Indeed, if you leave the gate open, He will come at the most inopportune times.

You see, it is our responsibility to open the gate to our garden because, if that gate is locked, it is latched from the inside. It's not that He doesn't want to come: It's not that He is withholding your Cheerios and giving the box, but you have not extended our bowl. You can't eat Cheerios without a bowl and He has put the bowl into our hands. God is not short on being found like a cupboard without supplies— certainly He knows where He is.

We cannot go to God. He is a spiritual being who lives in a spiritual house. We are a physical being and live in a world we can touch. He lives in a world we can't touch.

So, my friend, the bottom line is that if you feel you are separated from God by a wall, then it is because *your* gate is not open. Your *roast* needs to be tenderized and you need some *Cheerios* in your bowl.

Your soul is starved for that which is spiritual and your heart needs to become tender to the things of God. Ask. There is a lock on your gate that must be opened from the inside if you want the things of the Spirit to enter. It's not done in a physical world because the physical world does not connect with that which is spiritual.

If you open the gate to your heart (your garden) to the entrance of God, then He will come.

And, when He comes, what will He find? Is your heart hardened to conversation with Him? Do you already know what He will say, so you fill in the words? Are you afraid of Him? Will you provide a bench so He can stay? Are you so concerned with the weeds in your garden that you will rush Him to go so you can take care of things yourself?

He wants to be our friend. Imagine that—God wants to come to our garden and chat. He wants to speak to our heart. He doesn't use words—He's God. He uses spiritual language which we may be dull to comprehend.

And, if you have had your gate shut all this time; perhaps even built up a fortress against His entrance, dismantle it, open the door and say you're sorry. Greet Him before He enters. Don't wait to see the look of disappointment in His face…trust me….it will be too much. Just run to Him and apologize.

The one thing about God is that He does not go against His character—He is forgiving and ever loving. He will forgive and He will continue to love you. The difference is that now, you will feel it.

Pink Haired Girl

I gave my sweater to a girl with pink hair on the train because she
needed it. I was already warm enough and she had goose bumps
on her legs as she tried to sleep while we bumped along the
track toward our mutual destination. Why do you think He
gives
above and beyond?
So, we can give to those with pink hair.
But, remember, the pink hair does not
relate to their need. She was cold and did
not have a mom with her to give her one.
So I did. I was her mom for a few minutes.
And for a few minutes, she became my
daughter. A bond born by a need met.
That is how it is supposed to work.
But, we let other things get in the
way, things that never were
meant to get in the way.
Our pride, our selfishness, our apathy.
Major hindrances to the growth of kindness.
He has called us to be a family.
I don't really
Think we
know
what
that
means. Many of us never had
one. So, I guess we had better ask Him
about it. Because when I lent her my sweater,
It opened a way for a relationship of sharing. Then,
I wrote her a poem about how He loves those with pink
hair, as much as those who don't. And, she was touched to
the heart. So, was I. Because, even though I never knew her
name, she ministered to me. For, I saw in her the face of my
own daughter, who had been on drugs, on the street once.
I hoped that when she was cold, one day, someone had
given her a sweater when I couldn't be there to do it.

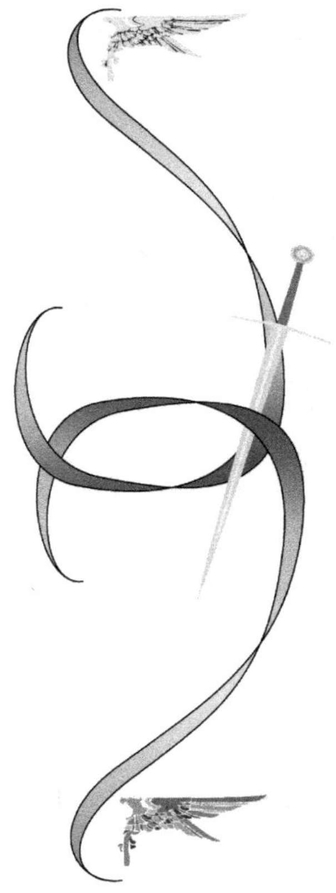

Chapters

Chapter I
Where God Isn't

In the Desert

To write this book I had to allow myself to feel the pain of separation from the one who created me.

I went to the desert and saw how dry it was. Even when it rained, it developed into a flash flood that did not profit the plants that grew there. It was dry, hot, and dusty. There was fine red silt that stuck to my socks, shoes and burned my eyes. There was no water except what I brought—what I carried. I brought cool water with me when I hiked.

Then I talked to Him. He was the only one there. Desolation and hunger is what I felt. My heart had been hardened by sin. I had built a garden on that rock. It was tender moss and delicate flowers that I showed to others. Then, I turned the rock over and grew some on the other side. But when I turned it over the moss on the bottom died. Each time I turned the rock of my heart over, a piece of me died. I was alive but dead. Living a lie, attempting to convince myself it was true. Where was truth? I could not face it. It was too brutal. I felt that it would destroy me; tear me to shreds and dismantle my personality.

I tried therapy spending $5000 going to someone with a fake name who charged me for advice causing me to divorce my husband leaving my children without a father.

I did not find God there—because He wasn't. He does not live in the places where we try to make excuses for going our own direction. He stands in the place where we left Him and sadly waits for realization to hit.

I followed my own ideas of who God was. I built an image of Him.
Then, I paid tribute to it. I sacrificed to my golden calf. I set it high on
a pedestal and encouraged those around me to serve it. But, it was not
true, because it was an image that I built myself. I had taken all of the
ideas that I held precious—all of my precious gold jewelry and formed
a beast. It never gave me anything back. It was a cow that gives no
milk—barren, just like the desert. It only stood in my path preventing
me from going the direction that I was supposed to go. My $5000 had
bought me an expensive statue. So, I fell down and worshiped that
beast.

You see, we have to fall down before we can worship. When we are
outside of the place where God intended us to be, then there is a lot of
tripping and falling. Then, when we trip, we think that we are out of
line with God, so we give. We give to a charity or a religious basket.
We try to spend more time with someone that we really hate. We press
ourselves into service for what we have come to worship. But, that
golden calf will give no milk. She can't. He will only reflect whatever
we have made him or her out of.

So, I came to the point where I was at the end of the rope dangling
over the fire. I could feel the flames lapping at my legs, ready to
consume everything that I had done in my life because none of it was
worth anything.

Then, I began to seek God on His terms, instead of my own. I will
never to assume understand how I became to know Him and hear His
voice clearly, but because He told me it is *possible* for others to do the
same, I share. My hope is, that no matter what your religious orientation
is, you will be able to value snippets of the voice from outside of our
world which has been retrieved by others throughout many years.

The inclusion of the holy books is intended to bring us from a place
we already know—a familiar voice—to permit more colors of the Spirit
to shine through. Be assured, the limitation of our faith in God [Allah] is
constrained by understanding of who we think Him to be. I have my piece
of the paper and you have yours. None of us has the whole paper. There is
no harm in being open to receive more of the spirit of who God is.

I have put, not only references to the holy books into this book,
but the detail of each, because I feel many may not own all of these
holy books, so it is by way of convenience that I include them. I went

to leaders of their specific faiths and requested the most accurate translations and versions of each.

Never in a million years do I assume to be qualified to release this book—and it has taken me 25 years to do so. I am not a holy book scholar or in an honored religious position. I am a seeker who has found something valuable—like gems waiting to be retrieved—and merely pointing them out to anyone willing to walk in the desert the same way I did. Be assured I put a lot of hours into detailed study of the holy books—but even more into conversation with my creator regarding the release of this book.

I can tell you assured that when I went to the Church of Latter Day Saints I found those seeking God.

When I went to the Catholic Church I found those seeking God.

When I went to the Mosque I found those seeking [Allah] God.

When I went to the Temple I found those seeking [YHWH elohim] God.

When I went to the Christian church I found those seeking God.

Consider—Is it the *same* God? That is why this writing is *A discourse through the reflection of five holy books.*

How did I get here? God told me to tell you. He carried me. I let go of the rope and fell into the fire. I turned myself over to His mercy. I decided that it was either true, or not. And, I pushed Him. I pushed God for the answer.

I stopped hiding my desolate heart from myself. I was the golden cow. I had glazed over what needed to be melted down to make the jewelry He wanted me to wear.

I cried out with everything I had. And I still do. I cry to my Creator for His mercy is everlasting and He does not withhold His love to us.

> We need only to ask forgiveness from our Lord; for He is oft-for-giving; He will send rain to you in abundance. [Surah 71.10,11, Qur'aan]

Then, I put the other distractions aside. I stepped out of all of the teaching that I had been given. I turned the television and the radio off. I quit reading the newspaper. And, I slowly turned my face toward Him. It was very painful as His light exposed the decay in my life. I turned a little at a time, as much as I could bear. The light was so bright that it hurt the heart.

But, just like a runner training for a match, each time I would push—push a little further in—into the light that exposed the pain that I had caused myself and my family.

That heart was so full of dark secrets of decay that I could see snakes come out of the holes like eels live in the shell of the coral reef. I was a coral reef, bones where life used to live. And the enemy had taken up comfortable residence in that place.

The light of God is like a fiber optic instrument. The channel of His light bends. The light does not bend but the channel of light bends in the hand of the great physician.

> He brings to light the things hidden since the beginning of time so that He can bring us healing and to Himself. [Colossians 1.25, New Testament].

> [If you pronounce the word aloud, it is no matter; for verily He knows what is secret and what is yet more hidden. Surah 20.7, Qur'aan]

So, I did nothing but voice my need to the Creator. I needed an infusion of a new life; I needed a transfusion of that which would bring life to my dead situation. I sought to live, not merely be alive. To walk, not merely stand. I could envision myself before the throne of the Lord when I die. I wanted to take care of the sin issue here on earth, so that when I am there, I could run to Him, not hide my face because of the sorrow over how I had lived my live. I didn't want to be one of those people who fall at this feet out of grief for what I had done and not done while here on earth. I wanted no regret. I wanted to set things up on earth so that I could be able to come to His face enter into His grace and be without regret.

But how? I threw down my tools. Everything I had. I was alone. No other person came with me. Just me and the Lord were there in the desert. And I threw abandonment to the wind. I brought my abandonment to Him and unleashed it.

Then, I prayed. I prayed Scripture. Verses, chapters, books. Every time I prayed for others, I prayed for myself. I sought His blessing in my life. I came abandoned and left the door to my heart open waiting for Him to show up when He desired.

And I kept coming back. Little by little the abandonment gave way to filling. The filling gave way to filled. The filled became overflow. Then, the top blew off the volcano. Lava spewed down to the sea.

He began giving me dreams and visions from heaven. They came like wonderful ribbons of light into the screen of my mind day and night.

I dared to believe the dreams were from Him. Then, I took a chance that visions might be true also. Never once did He disappointed me. They have all been true.

Then, He started to talk. It is not that He started to talk for the first time. It is that I started to understand what He was saying. I realized that He had been talking all along, but I never heard Him.

The voice of God comes to the heart, not the mind. He speaks to us as a child because that is what we are. He speaks to the heart, and then we must transfer the information to our mind to understand it. The transformation needs to be pure, unabridged, innocent, and tender like a small child responds to their parent.

It is like when I was a child asleep and my mother would tenderly come into my room and wake me. She would whisper. It would sink into my subconscious ears first, then work its way up to my conscious until I would wake up. The voice of the Lord comes that way. He whispers into our heart, then, it has to pass through to our subconscious. If there are blocks, then it will not pass through. We will not hear His voice.

If we want to hear God, clear out the blocks. Get rid of the dead wood in our life. Gather it up and burn it. It is the season to burn. In Washington there are a lot of trees. To clear the land they log the trees, pull the stumps, then, when it is burning season, they burn the stumps. We are logging the trees, confessing our sin, but we are not burning the stumps. We are not allowing the healing power of the Holy Spirit to infiltrate us and pull up the stumps. They have to be pulled up before they can be burned. This means visiting those painful experiences in our lives and opening ourselves up to receive his healing. It hurts, I know. But little, by little, the land will be cleared and make way to plant new growth. He wants to make us new. He wants to make new growth on our lot.

I have learned that God can be pushed. He will do a whole lot of clearing if we are ready for it. I believe He has an assignment held in His hand for each of us. It is up to us how fast we want to get to that place where we can do it.

Noah took his sweet time building the Ark. He could have done it much faster, but he didn't. [Genesis 6-8 Tanakh]

I got here in three years. I pushed. I pushed, and He pushed back. What I learned is that the Lord can be pushed: in fact He loves to be pushed. Did you know that you can change the mind of God? It's the only thing about Him that changes.

Amazing Faithfulness

His faithfulness does not depend on ours.

That is why they call it amazing grace.

The relationship is very uneven.

And He does not seem to mind.

Reasonable Relevance

Relevant, rational, reasonable.

Why are we so unreasonable when it comes to the

relevance of the rationality of the Truth?

The Lord is today as He was yesterday and will be for tomorrow.

He continues to be as relevant as He was ever since ever.

The break in the bridge happened when we became

irrational because we didn't see His reasons.

We couldn't reason our way to Him, so we declared

Him irrelevant.

Just because we can't see the bridge doesn't mean it doesn't exist.

Maybe we are the ones in the fog.

When did reason give way to relevance?

Death to a Cow

The Dream: *There is a brown milking cow on the trail. There is a brown leather coat over a wooden school chair. Death to a cow.*

Interpretation of the Dream: There was a cow in the Old Testament. It was a golden calf made by the Children of Israel. Moses and Aaron lead them across the Red Sea by the water parting. They end up in the desert encamped. Moses went up to a mountain to ask God what to do next.

He stayed gone for 40 days. Well, they don't know what had happened to him, so they stirred up their own plan of redemption. They melted down their jewelry and made a golden calf. They needed an image of the One who rescued them. They were desperate to serve the one who delivered them but, they did not know who He was. He had not revealed Himself to them for them to know Him. He tried. If you read the account, God invited all of them up to the mountain, but they were scared, and backed off. The only one brave enough to seek knowledge of Him was Moses.

The Children of Israel developed an image of God from what they knew. They were familiar with the gods of the Egyptians. But, lest we be too rough on them, notice that they did not make several cows. They only made one. They knew that He was supreme—that He was the God in charge of all.

We have cows. We have an image of who God is. This is whatever image that we have come to know. It is from our past; from what we have grown up with. The information is from our parents, school, holy books, and television. We set this image before us; on the trail, and we pay homage to it. We sacrifice to whatever image of God we have. Then we milk it. Milk is what flows from a cow. We drink whatever flows from the image that we have.

The second part of the dream has a leather coat on a chair. A leather coat is made from the skin of a cow. Obviously, this cow has been slaughtered. God wants us to sacrifice whatever image of Him that we have, back to Him. We need to give this image up. We need to ask Him to supply us with an image of who He is. He invites us each to come to His Mountain, as Moses did, and see Him face to face.

Has the story of Moses reached you? [Surah 20.9 *Qur'aan*].

He wants to talk to us and tell us who He is. When we come to Him and learn from Him, then our image will be accurate.

Then, our sacrifices will be acceptable to Him because they will be to Him, not another. [I Corinthians 2.10, *New Testament*] [Isaiah 64.4 *Tanakh*] [Enos 1.4-5 *The Book of Mormon*]

The leather coat is a representation of the coat of righteousness we need to wear to come into His presence. We need to put on the righteousness of our Lord given to us by His abundant mercy to be able to learn from Him. It is over a chair because when we take our seat at His table, it is like we sit down at the dining room table and talk with Him. We enter into communion with the Lord when we put our image of who we think He should be over the back of our chair. The only things we need to get the right image of God; are a leather coat and a chair. I believe we need to sit in the chair. It is a wooden chair used at school. We need to be schooled in who He is. Let Him talk. Ask.

Lopsided Relationship

When did we get confused and think we have to love

Him before He loves us?

Deal with it. The relationship with God isn't fair.

Victory

When you are not afraid to return to any place
along the trail of your life because God has walked
inside your heart to take you there, before now.
Back-track needs to be the track behind you.
Let it go. It was your rail before,
but not today.
Be healed,
O
dear
Ones.
Your pain
has more than crossed My mind. Oh that
the many names of God may be demonstrated!

Binding Love

The Dream*: There was a small booklet. At first it was bound with staples on the front. Then, it was bound with holes and three metal rings through the center of the whole stack of pages. Any page could become the front at any time. The binding is put on a certain way the book will open from both directions.*

Interpretation of the dream: Our lives are a book to be known and read by all men. We are the print of God that He gives to others. He wants to bind us His way. He wants us to own Him; to be His and have Him be ours. Give our heart to Him and ask Him to take it and make it new.

We have three parts to us; our heart, spirit and will. Often, we only recognize our heart and will. When we see someone we want to love, then we love him. The desire comes from our soul. Then, we tell our flesh to obey. We ignore our spirit. The Lord wants more. He wants all of us, in order. He asks us to give Him our will. We move toward Him by our desire. When we realize that we need Him, we kneel on the floor and ask for Him to be our Lord. Our will moves our flesh.

Then, when we ask the Spirit to help us, He changes us all around. The Spirit of God is a Spirit, so He cannot join with our flesh, He connects with our spirit. A new bond is formed that has never been formed before that day. God's Spirit joins with our spirit. When we ask for help through our spirit reaching out to the Holy Spirit, then He moves through us in a different way than we have ever experienced before. We learn how powerful our spirit is to direct us. It directs us through our heart melded to the heart of God. We become motivated by the love and mercy of God.

So, imagine how powerful it is when we ask Him to help us learn to love Him. Our drive, then activates our will; our soul. Our desire to please Him provides direction to our flesh. Our soul moves our feet to do what we tell them to do. We have become open and broken. When we became open to the Holy Spirit, He broke us apart. We became aware of our separate pieces. No longer do we have to be led by our will or our flesh, but we can be led by our spirit that is held in the hand of God.

Our Funeral

Does our memory of someone die at their funeral?

The bad seems to drift away

and the good stabilizes as we mull over their life.

Our only hope is the Lord will feel the same way at ours.

Time Coming

Time is like a bowling ball coming down the alley.

We are pinned. It will strike us

or will we be spared

its destruction?

Fallen from Grace

The dream: *There is a tall ladder that leads to a structure like a bill board sign. I climb it with my mother and someone else. Then, on the way up, I fall and scream, "AAAAH!"*

It's about 40 feet down. As I am falling someone yells to me to ask if I am OK. I yell back, "Don't worry, it happens all the time. I don't get hurt. Every day I stumble and fall. Fall from grace."

Interpretation of the dream: God has provided a series of rungs on the ladder of life for us. The steps are arranged a certain distance apart, but often we miss a rung on the ladder. We aren't paying attention when God wants to speak to us, so we don't know where the next step is. We get diverted and miss our step. Then, when we get to that place on the ladder, there is not rung for our foot to step on. We fall.

God has provided a safety net. It is like the rope that wraps around the waist of the person on the trapeze. It catches them when they fall so that they do not get hurt. God has provided us a safety rope—grace.

I think the others on the ladder are the prayers of my mother and an angel. Prayers can go before us and be beside us as we walk. They are very powerful companions to us in our climb up the ladder of life. Angels also stick pretty close to those close to God's heart.

To get the grace of God, we have to ask for it. It is not automatic, but by request. He always gives it. If we need more, just ask, He has an unlimited supply. He wants His work done.

Grace is like paint. God has the can in the garage. Whenever we feel the need for more, He will hand us the can. Suppose we get in a tight situation, we can call for more grace. Then we *can* go get it. The *can* comes to us. He paints the situation with the colors that He has in mind and we are able to pull through.

Often these difficult times are like mountains in our way. God does not move the mountain, but changes our outlook of it so that we are able to see where the tunnel is to get through to the other side.

I have worked for over 30 years as a nurse. Once, I received a patient to the Intensive Care Unit from the Emergency Room. She was a very old woman who had come from a rest home. Within 40 minutes, she went into a lethal heart rhythm and died.

Five minutes later, the front desk called me to report that she had visitors that wanted to see her. As I walked to the front to greet the visitors, I prayed for God to provide extra grace to me. It was a short prayer from my heart just before I opened the double electric doors that led to the ICU.

I had no idea who was on the other side of that door. It turned out that there were 5 huge people. They looked like football players to me. I tried to be gentle as I told them that their family member had just passed away, but when they understood the message they all let out blood curdling screams. They looked like they had all been shot. Staff came out of the surgery department to see what was going on in the hall. The family was completely overcome with grief. I stood there with my mouth open, and then started to pray for grace for them. As I prayed, they all calmed down.

Family members continued come to the hospital. As many as fifty came. God gave me the grace to minister to all of them amidst their grief. I had no idea that I was praying for the grace to minister to fifty grieving individuals when I prayed for grace. I presumed that I only needed a little grace. But God knew how much I needed, and He came through with what I needed.

The Holy Spirit brings not only power, but grace. Grace is the capstone to our relationship with God. It provides us with the ability to do things God's way instead of plowing through on our own. Grace makes it *OK* to fall from the steps and not worry about it.

A New Era

What is the difference between twilight and sunrise?
Look closely. The light is the same.
The air is cool. At sundown. There is a reflection of
the close of the day, Whereas sunrise
reflects the beginning of an era.
Both are held in the hand of the supreme God.

The Carpet Layer

When we die, will we rise to eternal life?
He says so, and He hasn't been wrong yet.
100% accuracy in predicting the outcome
of the future.
I guess, if the hand that rolls out the future
like a rug, is the same one that rolls it up,
I guess, He knows how it will lay out.

We Need His Molds

The Dream: *There are molds like the type to make ice cubes or play dough. They are on a stop sign in the middle of the road. Those traveling the road are to stop by in the center of the street to be molded.*

Interpretation of the Dream: Stop and press in; be pressed in. Man was made in the image of God. We reflect the image of God with our body. When we are saved by grace and enter into the family of God, we begin to reflect His image with our spirit and our soul. We become a three dimensional reflected image of God. Our spirit needs to commune with His Spirit and our soul needs to line up with His desires for us to be the correct reflection of His image. We have to learn Scriptures, listen to the Holy Spirit, and be obedient to what He tells us to do. This will cause us to be a 3-D image of the face of God.

Now Becomes Forever

Days, seasons, months, years.

Time.

When we let go of our own timeliness and

walk through His threshold, temporal becomes eternal.

Now becomes forever because we are living the Truth.

Rebuilding His Words

Why would it seem
strange that He breaks words apart
and rebuilds them the way He wants?
He did it with us.

The Potter

God molds us like a clay pot, not like a molten image. He places us onto the wheel, then works us with His hands, pressing and shaping. The motion is when the shaping takes place. The Kingdom of heaven is in motion. He adds water, to make us just the right consistency for whatever He is trying to build out of us.

A molten image is poured into a mold and set there until a specific time. It is abandoned until it cools down, then the inside is poured out. It is never touched by the master craftsman. When a molten image is made, it is left hallow inside. This is not the hand of God. This is an idol. It is a 3-D reflection of something other than God.

We have taken the work of God, us, and instead of attributing the work to the artist; we have given the credit to another. We have allowed another artist to sign the work of the hands of God. His art has been stolen. If we have been made like a pot by the hands of God, why do we give credit to others? He is the artist. We need to turn ourselves over to allow Him to autograph His work. Each one is an original work. Priceless. We are His vessels of mercy; and He raises us up to show His love. We are the reflection of His love for the world to see.

When God's wisdom flows from us it is like pure gold coming out of a chalice cup. God's wisdom looks like gold compared to clay within the values of this world. He declares that His values are with eternal things, not temporal.

God is looking for someone who will speak His words and not their own. Our own words are like making our own molds; our own idols. What happens is that when we say profound things, then we start to believe that these ideas are truth. Then, we build our lives on these words. When we do this we have made molten images and worshiped them. We have carved out our own path; with our own words because we have carved out our message on our heart.

When we use our own wisdom to run the kingdom of heaven, our words are worth no more than an earthen jar. We stunt the growth of our children when we feed them with the words of our own instead of those from God. Sometimes, we may think we are preparing God's food, but never go outside of the box we have built for Him within our own mind.

When we trust in our own self to come up with the answers, the logic
will collapse. It will smash just like a potter's jar. When we ignore
God's voice and follow our own, we will spend our life running from
Him. His voice pursues us. We will run until we are the only voice
heard.

No one will want to hear our voice except us because they will
be too busy listening to their own voices. We may climb our own
mountain; go to the place of our own dreams, but we will find
loneliness there because God won't be there. He is not in our own
dreams. He is in the dreams that He has for us—the best dreams for
our perfect happiness. And there He waits to bless us. We need only
respond to His voice.

Eternal Word

The Word of God is written clean across the pages of time.

He wrote the prelude and He is there for the addendum.

What happens in between is where we come in.

There is a chapter with our name on it.

What is on those pages?

Broken Communion Table

The dream: *I go to this lady's house. She lives near the sea. Everything I touch breaks. She's not happy because I keep breaking stuff, but she is building a new one. I lean on a table and it breaks. This happens three times. The husband comes over and looks at it. I say, "Of course, it broke three times. The leg was never firmly attached."*

The lady sends me away with gifts.

Interpretation of the Dream: The lady with a house near the sea represents the place where I see what God wants me to be and do. The woman is *mother wisdom* talked about in the book of Proverbs [Tanakh: Kethuvim, Proverbs 1-9 (the Writings)]. In the dream, I keep trying to do things my way instead of God's way.

I keep breaking stuff. What do I break? Everything I touch. God does not want me to get involved in the building of His heavenly kingdom. He wants to build His Kingdom, His way in His time. I break it all three ways. I try to do things my way, with my own strength and in my own time.

The table is the table of the Presence of God. It is the place where the bread is supposed to set. As I come into the presence of God, I can't even do that right. I keep trying to do it my way, my strength, and my time.

The dream has good news. The lady says that she is building a new house. I believe she is talking about me. She is building a new me that will be able to communicate with God His way, His strength, and in His timing. Of, course, the gifts are ours. God has given us gifts to help us get to where He wants us to be. He wants us to see.

When we rely on our own wisdom or the wisdom of others instead of listening to God, it will become a high wall that will crack, bulging and collapse suddenly in an instant. Only when we turn to God, and seek His ideas will we be able to move through life without breaking everything we come into contact with.

Often, we are so busy doing service *for* God that we don't take time to listen to Him. Often, when we try to love others, they do not love us back properly. Part of this web is that when we are disappointed, we drag others down with us. People that we know now, may not have met others who have hurt us, but they pick up the resentment toward them. Our new friend may hate our old friend, even without meeting him. The sin generates more sin between individuals that don't even know one another. *The splintered relationship becomes a reed that pierces a man's hand and wounds him if he leans on it. It puts slivers in the palm.*

God wants to break our heart. When we figure out what it means to break our heart, we will become close to where He wants us to be. He wants to separate us from ourselves. We need to separate the flesh from the spirit from the soul. We need to realize that He does not desire our flesh because it is dust, but He desires our heart and soul. If we say that we will give ourselves to Him, but hold back, then we are offering Him a partial sacrifice. We break off the pieces that we want to keep and give Him the rest. He wants to heal us completely, and He cannot if we are not willing to share the whole.

In the dream, the table breaks three times. God has responded to mankind three times, and all three times we have broken the communion table. We are the ones that break our deal with Him. We break off our leg of the table.

The first communion table was with Adam and Eve. There was a perfect world with Adam and Eve, but that communion was broken when they sinned.

The second communion table was when God came with the tablets and spoke to Moses. He looked for communion with a nation. He wanted them to become His country and His people. But, they turned their back on Him. They left Him standing there in the desert on a mountain. Only Moses came up the mountain to talk to Him when He invited the whole nation. Then, they followed Him for a while as He built a country out of them. But, if you continue to read the through Old Testament, you will see, when you come to the Minor Prophets, Israel left the communion of God.

One by one, God has sent prophets to help bridge the gap of communion with Him. He commissioned Elijah, Abraham, Jeremiah, Samuel, Mohammed, Moroni, Joseph Smith, John the Baptist, Jesus, and many more.

With each prophet, the people listened for a while, and then when their hearts began to become hardened, they rejected them because they did not like the message which refused to pamper their sinful life.

The third communion table was provided through His Spirit. We can commune with our spirit to His. He has made a provision to bridge the gap. And, to follow the dream, once again, we broke the table of His communion by refusing to listen to the *gentle voice* which He sends to give us guidance. He is as a spurned lover because, indeed, Our Lord is the lover of our soul.

These three legs build His communion table, but they are made of wood. In the dream, they are represented as wood, because we are as wood. Our bodies will not last, they will be made new. This world is fractured. The Lord will build a new communion table when He returns at the close of the age. There will be a new heaven and earth. This communion will not be broken because it is not made of wood.

References:

Do not offer to the Lord the blind, injured or the maimed or anything with warts or festering or running sores. Do not place any of these on the altar as an offering made to the Lord by fire *Leviticus 22.22* **Tanakh**

The Lord is close to the brokenhearted and saves those who are crushed in spirit. *Psalm 34.18* **Tanakh**

The sacrifices of God are a broken spirit; a broken and contrite heart, O God you will not despise *Psalm 51.17* **Tanakh**

He heals the brokenhearted and binds up their wounds. He determines the number of the stars and calls them each by name. Great is our Lord and mighty in power; His understanding has no limit. The lord sustains the humble but casts the wicked to the ground. *Psalm 147.3-6* **Tanakh**

His pleasure is not in the strength of the horse nor His delight in the legs of a man; the Lord delights in those who fear Him, who put their hope in His unfailing love. *Psalm 147.10* **Tanakh**

A happy heart makes the face cheerful, but heartache crushes the spirit. *Proverbs 15.13* **Tanakh**

A cheerful heart is good medicine, but a crushed spirit dries up the bones. *Proverbs 17.22* **Tanakh**

His legs are pillars of marble set on bases of pure gold. *Song of Songs 5.15* **Tanakh**

Therefore, this is what the Holy One of Israel says: "Because you have rejected this message, relied on oppression and depended on deceit, this sin will become for you like a high wall, cracked and bulging, that collapses suddenly, in a instant. It will break in pieces like pottery, shattered so mercilessly that among its pieces not a fragment will be found for taking coals from a hearth or scooping water out of a cistern. *Isaiah 30.12-14* **Tanakh**

Look now, you are depending on Egypt that splintered reed of a staff, which pierces a man's hand and wounds him if he leans on it! *Isaiah 36.6* **Tanakh**

"Speak this word to them: "'Let my eyes overflow with tears night and day without ceasing; for my virgin daughter—my people—has suffered a grievous wound, a crushing blow. *Jeremiah 14.17* **Tanakh**

Then I took my staff called Favor and broke it, revoking the covenant I had made with the nations. It was revoked on that day, and so the afflicted of the flock who were watching me knew it was the word of the Lord.
I told them, "If you think it best, give me my pay; but if not , Keep it" So they paid me thirty pieces of silver.
And, the Lord said to me, "Throw it to the potter"—the handsome price at which they priced me! So I took the thirty pieces of silver and threw them into the house of the Lord to the potter.
Then I broke the second staff called Union, breaking the brotherhood between Judah and Israel.
Then the Lord said to me, "Take again the equipment of a foolish shepherd. For I am going to raise up a shepherd over the land who will not care for the lost, or seek the young, or heal the injured, or feed the healthy, but will eat the meat of the choice sheep, tearing off their hoofs. *Zechariah 11.10-17* **Tanakh**

"Our Lord! We have heard the call of one calling (us) to Faith, 'You believe in the Lord,' and we have believed. Our Lord! Forgive us our sins, blot out from us our iniquities, and take to Yourself our souls in the company of the righteous.

Our Lord! Grant us what You promised to us through Your Messengers, and save us from shame on the Day of Judgment: for You never break Your promise." *Surah 3.193-194 Al-'Imran Qur'aan*

For, He is the same yesterday, today and forever: and the way is prepared for all men from the foundation of the world, if it so be that they repent and come unto him. For, he that diligently seeketh shall find; and the mysteries of God shall be unfolded unto them, by the power of the Holy Ghost, as well in these times as in times of ole, and as well in times of old as in times to come; wherefore, the course of the Lord is one eternal round.

And the Holy Ghost giveth authority that I should speak these things, and deny them not. *2 Nephi 10:18-19, 22* **Book of Mormon**

Now was the day of Preparation, and the next day was to be a special Sabbath. Because the Jews did not want the bodies left on the crosses during the Sabbath, they asked Pilate to have the legs broken and the bodies taken down. The soldiers therefore came and broke the legs of the first man who had been crucified with Jesus, and then those of the other. But when they came to Jesus and found that he was already dead, they did not break his legs. Instead one of the soldiers pierced Jesus side with a spear bringing a sudden flow of blood and water. *John 19.31-34.* **Christian New Testament.**

My Sticky Eyes from Disbelief

The Dream: *The Lord is waiting from the middle. My eyes are stuck from disbelief. They are hard to get open cutting through the middle.*

Interpretation of the Dream: The eyes of my heart are stuck. Eyes get stuck with matter. I am stuck from disbelief. I have to believe that the spirit world exists before I will be able to walk into it. God talks to the eyes of the heart. The eyes of my heart are stuck on what matters to my own heart, not His.

He is waiting in the middle. He wants to see others through the eyes of my heart, but it is hard because He is having to look through the matters of my own heart. It is like He is eyes in the middle of me wanting to look out. He is having to go through me—my Soul, my flesh and blood. When God looks at others, He goes through me, through my lifeblood. I am more concerned about my own life than His or others.

He is shining His laser out of my heart to others, but it is not the best. He needs me to remove what is sticky; to wash that matter from the eyes of my heart. If I don't wash it, it dries and hardens to become hardness of heart. Disbelief. Not believing in the promises of God. Not believing in the truth that there is a heavenly Kingdom on earth.

The Lord is in the center. I need to go to Him, confess my disbelief, and ask Him to give me belief in Him. He does not want to cut me; to break my chest and repair my heart with His knife. He does not want to do heart surgery on me, but He would rather have me come to Him for heart repair now. I need to lie on the table (like becoming a sacrifice on the altar), open myself to Him, confess my disbelief and ask Him to repair my sticky heart. I need to cry out for help.

God is forgiving and loving. He is waiting in the middle, like one waiting in the middle of the park for those who came along with him to return so they may continue their day in unity. He is waiting for us to return to Him. He cannot be anywhere but in the middle because He is a jealous God. He cannot share the middle with anything else that matters to us.

"Those who sustain the Throne and those around it sing Glory and Praise to their Lord: believe in Him; and implore Forgiveness for those who believe: "Our Lord! Your Reach is over all things, in Mercy and Knowledge. Forgive then, those who turn in Repentance, and follow Your path; and preserve them from the Penalty of the Blazing Fire!

"And grant, our Lord! That they enter the Gardens of Eternity, which You have promised to them, and to the righteous among their fathers, their wives, and their posterity! For You are the Exalted in Might, full of Wisdom...." *Surah 40.7* **Qur'aan**

I have been given tough messages for others which I have not delivered. I did not tell them because I was afraid of what they would think of me. I was also in disbelief. I did not believe that the message was actually from God. If I did, I would treat it as such. I would carry it with the same reverence that I carry my Scriptures.

I asked God, "Why did you tell me and not them? If the message is for them, why did you tell me?"

He said, "They won't listen. At least you listen. You may have some selective hearing going on, but you listen."

Then He said, "But you must be willing and obedient to do what I tell you to do. He who knows what to do, and does not do it, to him it is sin. You are disobedient because you have not delivered the messages."

He continued, "You appear to have faith because you have no problem interpreting the messages that I have given to you and making them for a larger group of people. You have no problem writing them down, and asking Me what they mean, but you have not given the message for the person whom it was intended. I have not come to call the masses, but individuals, one at a time. I thought you wanted to be part of the plan. Where are you?"

I have fogged over His issues with my own. There is a fog around my heart where it goes from the inside to the outside. I have focused on my own flesh and bones; saving my own skin, and this has caused the issues of God to become fogged coming to the outside. He needs me to become repentant, wash, and come to Him for help. The Spirit of God will help with my disbelief. I have to let the care for my own self go.

I got on the floor and repented. I asked for God to forgive and cleanse my soul.

He said, "Sheri, I can't give any more. I already have given everything I have. The ball is in your court now. I only ask for obedience. You said that you would. I am asking you to be true to your word. I understand you. It's OK. That is why I give My Spirit. Empty your cup; what you are holding, repent. Then take the cup that I have already given you. I gave it to you, but you set it back by the sink instead of delivering the food for whom it was intended. You signed up to serve. Now, do it."

So, I responded, "God, I love you. I love you. Please give me Your help. I am sorry for not carrying your messages to those for whom they were intended. Please forgive me and send that sin from as far as the east is from the west. I need You."

Then, I laid face down on the floor and asked Him to come into my heart and repair what was broken.

And He did. So, I turned up the music and praised Him for His loving kindness.

Chapter II
Kingdom of God

New Room: New Clothes

The dream: *I drove to my mother's house to attend a Tupperware party. There were several people there, including my mother and the atmosphere was casual and happy. When I got there, I realized that I was naked. The other people didn't seem to mind that I was naked and just wanted my company, but I felt uncomfortable. My mother was the same size, so I knew she would have something for me to wear in her closet. I went out of one door way, made a severe turn and entered into another doorway. There was a man clinging to me as I went out the doorway trying to get me to stay, but I assured him that I would return dressed for the party. As I entered through the door into the bedroom, I was instantly wearing a gorgeous blue angora sweater. I recognize this sweater because I wore it as a teenager, when I began serving God instead of others.*

I look around the room and find some pants hanging over a door. They are of a single thread knit with rows of pearls up the legs. They are bell bottoms and the bottom of them is a dark blue color with the color changing to lighter blue toward the waist. There are no seams in the pants. There was a design embedded in them, like an architect's plans for a building. The pattern was clear at the top, but difficult to see toward the bottom of the pants because the color was too rich.

I put the pants on and the seat fits perfectly. The only problem is that the pants were about 8 inches too long. And, then I notice that there is way that has been provided for the one who wears these pants to be able to walk without tripping. There is a channel with tiny holes embedded in each leg about 8 inches up which has a single lace threaded. When I pulled the leg up and cinch the lace, it makes the pants shorter and enables me to walk without tripping. The pants were elegant and when I put them on they matched the sweater perfectly. I realized that everything had been laid out ahead of time for me. I just needed to step into them.

Then, I turned for accessories to go with my outfit and there were several jewelry boxes laid out on the bed opened yet none seemed right for me. I knew that I would be given jewelry when it was time, later on.

Interpretation of the Dream: First of all, let me say that I wish every dream I had was like this one. What a wonderful dream! Thanks be to God for His wonderful visions into our mind!

The mother in my dream refers to *mother wisdom* spoken in Proverbs. The book of Proverbs uses a feminine noun to describe this aspect of God's character. God is not defined by our body, so we cannot say He is as we are. He has feminine characteristics of nurturing and *mothering* as well as masculine characteristics of protecting and providing. Proverbs uses a woman to depict the wisdom of God because the mother is usually the one who deals out the rules and raises the children to obey them. [Proverbs 8.1-4. Tanakh] She gives advice and training: so does the book of Proverbs. I don't believe, for a moment that God is a woman—or a man.

We should never presume to think He is as we are. Surah 55.1-7 *Qur'aan*

In the dream I am invited to attend a *party* given by my mother. When I go to the house of Wisdom, I see that what I am here for is a Tupperware party. (By way of explanation for those who are unfamiliar with Tupperware, it is a retail line of plastic containers which are used to keep food fresh. They were the first ones who invented containers which held food so it could be put into the refrigerator and kept fresh. They do not sell their product in the stores, but through a system of parties. When one woman has a party, she invites her friends and receives free Tupperware according to the volume of sales that is generated at the party. Then, hopefully, the representative can *cook up* another invitation for a party from some of the guests, to generate more sales for the future).

The correlation between a Tupperware party, wisdom and the invitation, is that we are all invited to attend a gathering sponsored by God—according to His character of wisdom.

It is like a party in that we can consider it fun and invite our friends to come along as well. The products which were offered at the gathering of the people brought together by Wisdom all have to do with keeping things fresh. Tupperware keeps its food fresh because it is sealed inside of a plastic container with a tight lid that snaps into place when it is put on in a specific manner. When we come to God and ask for His Wisdom, He provides the seal for our teaching and everything snaps into place. He is the one who seals His teaching in our lives.

Many refuse to accept words of prophecy given by those whom they do not know because they are afraid that the words are not from God. Also, many refuse to read *holy books* because they are afraid that the words might not be from God. But, according to this dream, God's Wisdom is the one who *seals* in the freshness of His words. He will seal in the words which we need keeping out that which defiles. We can trust Him to provide the means which brings discernment to be able to tell the difference between those things which are from Him and not from Him. *That is the spirit of discernment.*

What this section of the dream is telling us is that we can trust the Wisdom of God to seal in the words which are from Him and to seal out the ones which are not from Him. He is the One who places the seal on our heart, protecting it from wrong teaching.

In the dream, we are *all* invited. Indeed, every holy book which I have studied says that all are invited to share in God's Wisdom, yet we have chosen to use our own instead. And, every holy book, then, goes on, with long dissertations, to instruct on how to get back to the place where we can receive His Wisdom and Understanding.

Back to the dream: When I arrive, I realize that I am naked. What this means is that when I come to the place where the Wisdom of God resides, I realize I have none. What I have done up to this point is to rely upon my own. So, it is like being naked: I must leave all of my *adornment* and take up that which is provided for me. In the dream, I leave the gathering and go out one door and into another. We must leave our own wisdom before we can enter into the area of putting on the Wisdom of God. Others think we are OK, but if we ask God, He will show us where we stand. In the dream, others were happy to accept me and allow me to stay at the party when I was naked; even clinging to me when I wanted to put on some clothes. However, I knew something was wrong, so I decided to leave and return when I was appropriately dressed. It would be a dishonor to my mother to arrive at her party without the proper clothes on.

There is a reference in the New Testament which refers to the End Times when we will all face judgment. It is a parable which correlates being invited to a wedding, yet not being properly attired. In the parable, the ones who arrive without wearing wedding clothes are thrown out and the door is locked behind them. In the New Testament, the wedding refers to the marriage of the Church to Christ as a husband and a wife. In essence it is saying that when the times are fulfilled and Jesus returns to become joined with the Church, he will invite guests to the ceremony. They need to be properly attired, or they will be thrown out onto the street and the door will be locked. (Matthew 22) The correlation for New Testament Christians is that they need to be prepared when Jesus returns to gather the Church.

The Islamic teachings of Mohammad have a similar instruction in that they teach that, by following the five pillars of the faith, one can be prepared when the time of judgment comes. The five pillars are faith, prayer, fasting, zakat (giving of alms) and Hajj (pilgrimage to Mecca). One of Islam's major goals is that mankind should live in remembrance of that Day when all will be assembled before God. (ref. *Islam as it is*.)

Back to the dream: When we enter into the place of adornment of the Wisdom of God, we must make a sharp turn in our thinking. I went from one place to another entering out of one doorway and into the next. Notice that everything was already laid out for me: I just needed to step into it. God has what we need already laid out for us. Some of what I needed was laid over a door and other things were laid on the bed. Part of what we need to learn comes to us as we enter into different areas in our life. Other things can be learned through hearing His voice in dreams, visions and gentle listening of the whisper into our soul— laying on the bed.

As I stepped into the pants, they were already imprinted with *blue prints* for walking. God has the blueprints for our lives: we simply need to put them into action. We need to step into what He tells us to do—become obedient to His voice of Wisdom. The pants are too long for me. When I put them on, if I don't make special provisions, I will trip around. When we step into the blueprints of God, we need to use what He has provided within the plans to prevent us from stumbling. There was woven into the fabric of the plan a way which would keep me from tripping as I learned to draw upon His provision (cinch it up.) I think the provision might be using His grace and mercy through the forgiveness which is freely given.

In the last part of the dream I see several jewelry boxes on the bed, but realize that there was no jewelry to go with my outfit. Jewelry is often called *accessories* to an outfit. What I see within the dream is that although the *outfit* is all laid out for me in the room of *Mother Wisdom* my accessories will come later. God gives the jewels of knowledge, like gems of understanding regarding specific principles along the way as we need them. He provides specific enlightenment which adorns our ears, our neck and our wrists that go with specific situations. It is like wearing an outfit, but sometimes wearing different jewelry dependent on the occasion. He will give our ears specific understanding to know certain things when we go to certain places—open our spiritual ears to understand. He will give us ear –rings: He calls us then and there.

A necklace refers to a covenant because it encircles our neck passing from our body to our head. When we are committed to understanding things from His vantage point, He gives l guidance related to the covenants which we have already made with Him and our faith— whatever it may be. We limit God when we insist that He only works to provide guidance within the one we are in. God is much bigger than that. He can bring guidance through any religion where He is the center focus. In the dream there is no jewelry for me in the boxes on the bed—in essence there is nothing for me when I am boxed in by my own views. I must go to the party of Mother Wisdom and receive there.

Additional References: Psalm 25.5 **Tanakh,** *I Corinthians 12.4-9, I John 2.26-27* **Christian New Testament,** *2 Nephi 27.34-35* **Book of Mormon.**

A New Hope

There
is a new hope
in things that we
never thought could be true.
They thought they were only fantasy. The ability to hear My
voice for themselves. But, now they know I am able to be
heard. And, I have revealed it to them in a way that
they can grasp. I have put it into their hand.
The prayers
of my people have been heard.
Walls were up. I could feel them.
I felt their anger and abuse.
But, I am here to tell you that they are coming down.
Broken hearts to be mended through hope of who I truly am.
It is not about who others think I am. It
is about who I really am.
I will tell the people
Myself.
Inspiration
has come to My people.
By this word they will ask Me.
Now, they know they
can.
It is
a mystery
of faith. Now
revealed. A promise fulfilled.

Highway to Holiness

The highway is hearing the voice of God. The road must be prepared. The obstacles must be removed out of the way for God's people. God's voice calls to prepare His people for the way, the straightway in the wilderness, a highway for our God. (Isaiah 40.3) **Tanakh**

We cannot go there. His voice comes to us. When we hear the low tones, it is the gentle voice within our spirit. The things of God that are too lofty, magnificent and awesome God will bring to our level of understanding. His thundering voice He will make to be at our level; a level of understanding.

Certainly Moses knew God and went to His house.

> When Moses came to the place appointed by Us, and his Lord addressed him, he said: "O my Lord! Show (Yourself) to me, that I may look upon You." Allah said: "By no means can you see Me (direct); but look upon the mount; if it abide in its place, then shall you see Me." Surah 7.143. **Qur'aan**

When His voice is clear to us, then we will begin to understand the His mind. He will be able to provide us with counseling, enlightenment, direction and knowledge of Him. He will be able to show us the pathway of understanding Him.

Without His insight, our minds are totally unable to comprehend God's ways. We cannot fathom His mind. In our desperation to know Him, we improvise with other things that we focus our attention on.

God hates this. It's like going to a third person to learn all about the one who loves you, yet never going to the one who has given everything to be with you. Go to God. Listen to His voice. Learn from Him. He will provide a highway of information about Himself if we can only learn to listen to His voice.

The Highway to Holiness is a river. It flows from the throne of God. The account of heaven depicted in the book of Revelation in the Christian New Testament is awesome. Let me encourage you to read it.

"At once I was in the Spirit, and there before me was a throne in heaven with someone sitting on it. And the one who sat there had the appearance of jasper and carnelian. A rainbow, resembling an emerald, encircled the throne…" Revelation 4.2-3 **Christian New Testament**

We walk in it as we wear the robes of righteousness which He provides. We cannot bring our own because we have been born of this world, not from above. Praise God He has given us a spiritual connection to enable us to connect with Him.

Additional References: Proverbs 1.28-32, Proverbs 15.24 **Tanakh,** *1 Nephi 17.46* **The Book of Mormon**

Lord,

Please show us the pathway to understanding You.

Give us the righteous robe that only flows from heaven.

Paving the Road

He paves the road way with His steam roller.

The power of God moves with His word when we pray into the will that He shows us.

He will pave the way for us.

The intentions of the enemy are covered over with cement.

They can no longer stand in your way.

Everything moves out of the way when a road is built. Property is purchased because individuals need to move over to make way for new development of the city.

God has a city, a Kingdom. He has roads to it that He wants to pave.

He paves them with His purposes.

Everything that leads to Him has His holy intentions in mind as well. There are rest stops along this road, restaurants, shopping plazas, and houses.

He will pave the way for us to get to all of the blessings that He has already intended us to get to.

It is as if they are within a place where no road has reached, as yet. He wants to pave a road to that city.

Our prayer paves the road with eternal stones and provides a way for us to, not only walk but move the vehicle that He has given us, on.

The vehicle is our spiritual gifts within the package, He gives. If it is wisdom, then He may give us a package of speaking.

He may also give us the package of writing.

He may give the package of singing of His true character. These are all vehicles that He provides to move along the road that He paves.

When we pray for Him to open the way, then get into the vehicle, we can move at a rapid pace down the road of Holiness as He makes all of the lights green.

We must remember, however, that the road is made of fresh tar and it is hot. The fire of God by the power of the Spirit is what paves the road.

We can only walk on hot surfaces when we wear the protective shoes which are provided for us.

Many prophets have left foot prints. We can follow their trail, or ask for our own to be shown. If He has shown them the way, will He not also show us?

Indeed, God will provide us with shoes which enable us to walk through the fire to get to the place where He dwells.

We can put on His sandals and adorn our feet with righteousness.

Only when we are clothed with the righteousness of God, can we walk into His city.

Light for the Path

The Dream: *There is a car with pop up headlights. The headlights are stuck in the up position.*

Interpretation: God has given us the vehicle to see into the dark where we are going. He wants us to always have our *eyes* open in front of us. The *eyes* that He responds to are not the ones in our head, but the vehicle that He has given us—a heart to seek Him.

The direction that God provides to us is not for our feet like a camper with a flashlight on a trail. The path that He lights for us is for eternal direction. He is more concerned with long term issues than with the things that will be history next year.

When we are motivated by the love of God for others, we will be directed in all of our steps because they can't be wrong. Whether we step to the right or the left, people will be blessed through us.

God reveals His plan to us into our heart. Our spirit needs to be taught how to listen to our heart so we can understand what it is and do it. Then, when He talks to us, we should cherish those words. Write them down and ask Him to help us understand them. What do they mean? Only He can interpret what He has put on our hearts. God will enlighten us; we don't have to try to do it on our own. Just ask Him. We can ask for wisdom and understanding. God has provided us a window through His Spirit speaking in a gentle voice into the core of our being.

> The Lord does choose you and teach you the interpretations of stories and perfect His favor to you and to the posterity of Jacob – even as He perfected it to your fathers Abraham and Isaac aforetime! For Allah is full of knowledge and wisdom *Surah 12.6* **Qur'aan**

He will not reveal His will for us to our mind. Our mind needs to be taken out of the loop. What God tells our heart to do provides the direction for our path.

Everyone's spirit has eyes, not just those claiming to be *baptized and filled* with the Holy Spirit. God has given everyone spiritual eyes so that others can tell when someone is sad or happy without them saying anything. We can sense the spirit of another person. It is like their *spirit* eyes can see into our *spirit* eyes. We are like two cars meeting on a dark road; our headlights flash at one another. When our eyes shine with the Love of God to others, they will see Him as they look into our eyes.

Additional References: Psalm 19:8, 119:18, Proverbs 4:20-25, Isaiah 29.10, 40.26, Isaiah 52.8-15 **Tanakh,** *Matthew 5.29, Luke 11:34, I Corinthians 2:9, Ephesians 1:18, 6:6* **Christian New Testament,** *Surah 16.30* **Yusuf Qur'aan**

God de Light

Delight is the key.

De light.

Like creamer. Be stirred. Be light.

By His delight to you, in you, through

You and back. Stirred around and back to Him.

It's like a chocolate dipped

spoon that flavors coffee.

Where's My delight?

In you.

The Kingdom of God— A Picture

The dream: *There are two houses with a street between. On one side is the house called **Wisdom** and on the other side of the street is one called **Knowledge and Understanding**. The road between them is the **Highway to Holiness**.*

Interpretation of the dream: God has provided a neighborhood in the Kingdom of God. It is waiting for us to become one of its inhabitants. The house of Wisdom is on one side of the street. It is the love relationship that we build with God through His grace reaching out to us.

The house on the other side of the street is one called Knowledge and Understanding. Knowledge is when we learn about God—who is He? Understanding is where we learn why He is the way He is.

The street is the Highway to Holiness. It is when we follow the voice of God that we can walk into the level of Holiness that He desires. Holiness is a progressive walk toward God until we reach absolute holiness when we enter into His final presence in the heavenly places. We seek God's help here on earth through the power of the Holy Spirit to enable us to become more like the person He desires us to be, then we walk down that road toward greater holiness and purity.

The throne of God is at the end of the street. The street in the dream symbolizes the flow of the Holy Spirit from the throne of God. It is His outward flow of love and colorful rainbow light—inspiration of God is brought to us by a flow from Him. We cannot learn anything of God without Him bringing it to us because we are held in a physical space. Only when He reaches out to us, can we enter into the spiritual realm. Once we get onto the road to holiness, it is His edict that we should walk in it toward Him. And, how do we know the way? Just like someone who cannot see, but can only hear—we must go to Him directed by the sound of His voice.

The dream sounds like a game of Marco-Polo that children play in the swim pool. They have teams who get on someone's shoulders and hold their hand over the eyes while the other team calls out, "*Marco,*" the responder calls out, "Polo" enabling the team to get together and win the game. God is calling out to our spirit with His. As we respond to the *call*, He calls again to help us get our bearings and be directed toward Him. We cannot see Him, so we must learn to listen to His voice with our spirit to be enabled to find Him.

As I meditated on the dream, The Spirit showed me that there is a sky bridge which connects the two houses. A sky bridge is a glass structure that goes between the houses of Wisdom and Knowledge with Understanding over the Highway to Holiness. This sky bridge is called *Inspiration.* It is the insight into spiritual things which enables us to link the houses together in our mind.

The whole picture must be in complete cooperation to enable us to see things according to God's vantage point. Only as we stand on the road of Holiness and link to all of the houses (wisdom, knowledge and understanding) will we become enabled to see the *inspiration*. It is the link to *why* things happen a certain way in our lives and those around us. For it is by *inspiration* that spiritual things of God make sense for us today. I like the sky bridge.

The Neighborhood of God's Kingdom

The picture that He paints throughout the book of Proverbs is a neighborhood of elegant mansions. These brick mansions were built long ago by a single builder. They have placards in the front yard with endeared names for each one. The yards are carefully manicured. There are all sorts of beautiful trees; mighty oaks, cedars from Lebanon, and towering Firs to name a few. They are all pruned every season as needed by the gardener. The window boxes have flowers all the colors of the rainbow. There are the beautiful red Roses of Sharon and the pure white Lilies of the Valley. Every house has fruit trees and grape arbors. The gardener loves to cross pollinate the fruits to make new varieties each season. He brings the grapes to the winery and they produce the finest wines ever.

There are no sidewalks in this neighborhood. It was built in a time before anyone had any place else to go. There are walkways that lead to each house from the roadway. They are the work of a jeweler. They are made of gold and silver with inlaid gems. Each house is identified by the colors of the gems in the walkway leading to it. The gems reflect the brickwork of the Mansion. The street between the mansions is so narrow that a person can nearly reach out and touch another from the upper story leaning out the window of each house. It is paved of solid Gold that reflects the sun like glass.

When the sun shines in this neighborhood, it is very bright and will blind someone who doesn't have eye protection. All of the residents have special sunglasses to give them the ability to see the way home each day.

House of Wisdom

The house called Wisdom has rubies the shape of apples embedded in gold and silver that are in the pathway. Each of the houses has its own *Welcome Wagon Woman* to help introduce the house to others. She shows visitors around the place. She doesn't own the mansion, but serves the needs of the owner and the house with delight. She is almost a personification of the house she lives in because she has been there so long.

The *Welcome Wagon Woman* of the House of Wisdom is a plump lady. She is kind and loving to all that come to her house. She wears full length dresses that are pure white and have strands of pearls from her head to her feet. She has a wonderful necklace of silver that hangs down over her heart. It has a gold apple with a small hinge that allows the apple to open up. She keeps within it a picture of her Master.

House of Knowledge

The house of Knowledge has many windows. It has a large basement where the children can play freely. It has skylights in all of the rooms. They are filled with light. The skylights are special. They retain the light passing through, so that even at night, it is like daytime within this house.

The tool shed is filled with the most magnificent tools. The shovels have handles of made of titanium with diamond blades at the end. There are tillers and post hole diggers made of the finest, hardest metals. All are shined spotless. The gardener washes each tool after use and puts it in its spot in the work shed.

The kitchen has every utensil needed to cook the most elegant meals.

All of the knives have diamond tips. They sit near the pot belly stove. The people of this house usually eat in the kitchen at the picnic style table. Sometimes they take food to their rooms at night.

There is a wing with a library. Gold filigree books from floor to ceiling adorn this library. Often, those in the house need to stretch to reach a book to read. A movable ladder is there, so they can get to the hard to reach ones. There is a heart shaped sofa covered with lamb's fur and a coffee table in the center of it. It has a glass top with halite crystals as legs.

The woman of this house is old. She walks with a walker. Even though she is slow, she will always answer the door when someone visits. They never lock the door—it is always a little ajar. To come into this house, visitors step into the threshold, yell, and then proceed. When they step over the threshold, a laser light announces their arrival. Those in the house will come to greet you.

Many rooms haves large hand carved beds and beautiful tapestries of gold, silver, blue and red. At the foot of each bed is a hope chest filled with treasures. The owner of the house travels abroad and brings back treasures to put into these chests. Anyone who stays in the rooms can take whatever treasure they want with them.

Personification of Wisdom, Understanding and Knowledge according to Proverbs, Job, Song of Songs. ***Tanakh***

Chapter III
Seven Spirits of God

The Lamp Stand

A shoot will come up from the stump of Jesse; from his roots a Branch will bear fruit.

The Spirit of the Lord will rest on him, the Spirit of wisdom and of understanding, the Spirit of counsel and of power, the Spirit of Knowledge and of the fear of the Lord, and he will delight in the fear of the Lord.   *Isaiah 11.1-3 **Tanakh***

The seven Spirits of God which are outlined in Isaiah are the presence, the wisdom, understanding, counsel, might, power, knowledge, and the fear of the Lord.

The **Presence** of God is when He shows up bringing His Spirit. The children of Israel followed the *manifest* presence of God in the desert when He led them by a cloud in the daytime and a pillar of fire at night. During that time, the presence of God was demonstrated in thunder and lightning with smoke and a trumpet sound. (Exodus 19.18 ***Tanakh)***

In Exodus 33, the Lord, Himself speaks about His presence going with them and providing that which brings rest. In that same portion He continues to say that when His goodness passes in front of them it is a demonstration of His mercy and compassion.

In the New Testament the Spirit comes to Jesus as he is baptized by John the Baptist in the river. The Spirit comes in a symbol of a dove accompanied by a voice from heaven—recognized by others as coming from God. (Mark 1.11 ***Christian New Testament)***

In the *Testimony of the Prophet Joseph Smith,* he relates a story of an appearance of exceeding whiteness, a person whose description was glorious beyond description having a countenance like lightening. Written in the *prelude* to the **Book of Mormon**, the heavenly being describes himself as Moroni.

Let us consider the encounter which Joseph Smith had in his bedroom was so profound that he went on to write it down and move many people toward a faith in believing it as true. It is very difficult to deny what he saw was a godly form sent from heaven carrying a presence which we cannot know on earth unless it comes from above. (*Testimony of the Prophet Joseph Smith* **Book of Mormon**)

Oh, and I will be dull if I do not mention that the Holy Book **Qur'aan** speaks of Moses' encounter with the fire. It reminds us that Moses obtained guidance at the fire when a voice was heard.

> "Verily I am your Lord! Therefore (in My presence) put off your shoes: you are in the sacred valley Tuwa. I have chosen you: listen then, to the inspiration (sent to you). *Surah 20.9-13* **Qur'aan**.

Two other Spirits of God are **Wisdom** and **Understanding**. A spiritual definition of Godly Wisdom is to have the mind of the Lord in such a way that decisions are made based on relating to things from this perspective. Certainly, none of us can argue that God is the most wise One.

When I first became acquainted with the English Interpretation of the **Qur'aan** which I was given by a kind friend who sensed my desire to understand his faith, I was impressed by a symbol in the front of the book. After I fasted through Ramadan Season and attended the Mosque for the services, I asked a spiritual woman who spoke the language fluently what the symbol meant. She said that it meant, the many *beautiful names for God*. This symbol is on the first page of the book. How wonderful to begin the study of the principles of the Wisdom of Allah by recognizing that He has many names.

Hands of Grace

Held in my hand, tucked in the plan
between the fingers tips of another.
Held by my Lord, not my brothers
Hands of grace forsake me not
Envelop, develop, and renew what's askew.
Fill my in between places with Your faces
sandwiched in the fingers of Your graces.

Many Faces of God

This is a story of a recent encounter with a young Hindu lady. She was troubled by a dream and sent to me for interpretation.

The Dream: *I go to the place where our family usually worships and I see the face of another statue embedded in the face of the God which my family worships. In our place of worship there are many statues. Our family only worships one. All at once when I look at our statue, it has another face—one of the nearby statues is over top of its face. Those nearby can't see it as I can. It is truly amazing. With this new experience, I pray for power to be given to me which may bring healing and comfort to many through my hands. When I pray, I am given a special impartation.*

Interpretation of her dream: Within the God which you worship, He is showing you a different face.

Then, I asked, "What are the names of the statues."

She said, "The God which my family worships is one that is called by the name ***Incarnate***—meaning that he was a man at one time, but remained God. The other one is called by the name ***sustaining life***."

Based on this information, I further interpreted her dream this way, "Within the statue of the God you worship, He wants you to also see *His face* as the One who sustains life bringing power to heal and comfort. It is like seeing another face of God, but in essence it is the same God only from a different vantage point."

I am a nurse who understands EKGs. The dream correlates to an EKG in that it provides a 12 view picture of the heart. It is not 12 different hearts, but a variety of views which provide a larger picture of what is going on with the same heart. God wants to provide us with different views of who He is—not for the purpose of exchanging the view but expanding our understanding of who He is.

Let me tell you that this young woman was very excited because she longed to bring comfort and healing to others. In response to the dream, I gave her a copy of the book ***Tomaseña*** (one of my books) which speaks of the indwelling power of the Spirit to bring healing and comfort. For, I would be remiss if I did not mention that Comforter is another name for God—One of His many beautiful Names. The dream helped to open her understanding of that which was her desire.

The next day she brought me another dream.

The Dream: *I am at a Mosque and the people are all bowing and praying. But, the God which they are praying to has the face of the one which I worship.*

Interpretation of the dream: I told her that her dream means is that the Muslims are worshiping the same God which you are.

That very moment, her image of God grew even more.

The Fear of the Lord

I think of our understanding of God as a dot-to-dot picture. We are given dots—religious teaching and experiences. Somehow, in our finite mind we must connect those dots to provide a reason for our existence. Some pride themselves in the finished picture of their connected dots and parade it before others. To them it is profound—surely their picture leads the parade. Then there are others who portray humbleness neglecting to attempt to connect the dots. Their picture misses crucial element. Are they neglectant in their spiritual search or afraid of the answer?

> The fear of the Lord is the beginning of wisdom, and knowledge of the Holy One is understanding. Proverbs 9.10 *Tanakh*

Adhere that understanding the fear of the Lord is one of the most essential elements to spirituality. Indeed, the reference above indicates it is, not only pivitol, but the stone which three aspects of God's character rest upon—wisdom, knowledge and understanding.

Just a minute. How many are there in the seven spirits of God? Let's review.

- Wisdom—seeing things from God's perspective.
- Presence—when He shows up.
- Understanding—having things make sense.
- Counsel-decisions based on seeing from God's perspective.
- Might—the power of God.
- Knowledge—learning.
- Fear of the Lord—embracing God; rather than running

The verse in Proverbs indicates there is a building process. I believe knowing God is similar to knowing a person. First we meet him or her than spend some time together learning about each other. We share at increased levels as we come to trust. I think what the verse is indicating is that someone can never enter into a place of trusting the other person if he or she does not overcome their fear of opening themselves up. It's about opening up our heart to receive love. God is love and He is perfect. Both of these are included in His many beautiful names.

Therefore the love He shares with us is no less than perfect love.

Why do we run from the love of a person on earth? Most likely we have been hurt by others and fear a repeat of what happened prior. We say, "No way. I am not going to go through the pain. I will keep my heart closed and protect it from suffering."

Does it work?

Just the opposite. We suffer when we cannot find someone to love and be loved. Our heart has been created to be loved. The fear of the Lord is the love of God directed toward us.

The challenge is that it pivots on like a teeter-totter with justice. The justice of God demands payment for sin. Some religious influences focus on the justice of God with an attempt to *scare* others into their religion. While others neglect the justice aspect of God drawing many portraying Him as a *benevolent father who will overlook bad behavior.*

Fear of the Lord recognizes that holy God is, not only just, but desires to reach out with love. This is mercy, my friend. The first verse of the Qur'aan.

> In the name of Allah, Most Gracious, Most Merciful. ***Al-Fatiha*** 1.1 ***Yusuf Qur'aan***

To fear God is to know His character enough to understand He requires payment for sin because He is holy. Absolute holiness requires justification for sin in order for *sinners* to come close to Him. The priests understood this when carrying out their duties in the temple in times of old as written in Exodus.

> "Make the robe of the ephod entirely of blue cloth, with an opening for the head in its center. There shall be a woven edge like a collar[a] around this opening so that it will not tear. Make pomegranates of blue, purple, and scarlet yarn around the hem of the robe, with gold bells between them. The gold bells and the pomegranates are to alternate around the hem of the robe. Aaron must wear it when he ministers. The sound of the bells will be heard when he enters the Holy Place before the Lord and when he comes out so that he will not die. Exodus 28:35 ***Tanakh***

"According to Jewish tradition, one end of the length of the rope was tied to the high priest's ankle and the other end remained outside the tabernacle. If the bells on his robe stopped tinkling while he was in the Holy Place, the assumption that he had died could be tested by pulling gently on the rope." The NIV footnote for Exodus 28:35.

The question to considered is how does the fear of the Lord relate to wisdom and knowledge? Here is the answer that I received when I meditated on the question.

The *fear of the Lord referred to in Proverbs* is one likened to that which we have for someone that we love intensely. Love and fear are related.

The word says, "The Fear of the Lord is the beginning of wisdom."

The Fear of the Lord is **Shock and Awe** of God. Fear as *we know* it is **dread** that has to do with harm and destruction. To fear God is to realize that He is all powerful, and awesome, yet instead of running from Him, we run to Him. If there is an entity with potential to destroy us with it's breath, then the normal reaction is to run from it.

Consider—what if perfect love casts out fear...

There is no fear in love [dread does not exist]. But perfect (complete, full-grown) love drives out fear, because fear involves [the expectation of divine] punishment, so the one who is afraid [of God's judgment] is not perfected in love [has not grown into a sufficient understanding of God's love]. I John 4.18 **Christian New Testament Amplified Edition**

Names of God related to love appear across faiths, with Yahweh (the covenant-keeping God in Judaism/Christianity), Allah (specifically Al-Wadud, The Most Loving in Islam), and Hindu deities like Krishna, Radha, and Kamadeva (god of love) embodying divine affection, while Agape is the Greek term for God's selfless love in Christian theology, highlighting love as a core divine attribute. **AI Overview on Names of God, love.**

Have you ever been in a relationship and the other person loved you more than you loved him or her? As you grow closer, you become afraid of baring your heart. You are overcome by fear of intense love.

You duck out of the relationship because you are not ready for the intenseness of it.

Wisdom is defined as seeing things from God's point of view. Knowledge is knowing. So, if you put these two elements together—the definition of the fear of the Lord is knowing how God feels about you and seeing it from His point of view. Simplified in the paragraph above, you become *afraid* of the intensity of relationship—it is too much, so you recoil from it. It's like, "Whoa. I never knew how He felt about me. It is very hard to handle."

The emotions become overwhelming.

Looking at a human relationship of someone who is coming toward you with an overly intense love, then, you begin to self-examine and consider that no matter how much you love that person, he or she will always love you more. We *fear* because of the intensity of the relationship and their demands. Does he or she expect the same level of intensity in return?

So, the Fear of the Lord is to know the heart of God and to approach Him with reverence, awe and thankfulness because of the love that He has for us. Only through His love and mercy sin is atoned for.

> Limitless is your Lord in His mercy 6.147 *Qur'aan*

> In Islam, God's (Allah's) mercy (Rahmah) is central, encompassing His boundless compassion, forgiveness, and sustenance for all creation, expressed through names like Ar-Rahman (The Most Compassionate) and Ar-Raheem (The Most Merciful). *Al Mercy in Islam*

One who has learned to fear God has both righteousness and wisdom. When we start to learn the heart of God, then He will tell us His plans. This is wisdom. We are to be *zealous* in love with Him—He is for us. When we have no fear of anything, but Him, then we know that we are there. No fear of man or life, just God—who we see as love flowing through to us. Then we have entered into His rest. Because perfect love casts out fear.

Such love has no fear, because perfect love expels all fear. If we are afraid, it is for fear of punishment, and this shows that we have not fully experienced his perfect love. I John 4.18 ***Christian New Testament***

The correlation is that when we move toward God regardless of the consequences and open ourselves up to Him, our journey of *wisdom* begins. Wisdom flows from this relationship with God. It's like when we are in love with someone. We learn their heart; they learn ours and we delight in each other.

When he prepared the heavens, I [wisdom]was there: when he set a compass upon the face of the depth: When he established the clouds above: when he strengthened the fountains of the deep: When he gave to the sea his decree, that the waters should not pass his commandment: when he appointed the foundations of the earth: Then I was by him, as one brought up with him: and I was daily his delight, rejoicing always before him; Rejoicing in the habitable part of his earth; and my delights were with the sons of men. Now therefore hearken unto me, O ye children: for blessed are they that keep my ways. Hear instruction, and be wise, and refuse it not. Proverbs 8.27-33 ***Tanakh***

The Spirit of His Wisdom was in place when He set the heavens in place, when He marked out the horizon on the face of the deep. He had to have a plan to do this. Wisdom was the craftsman at God's side as He created the earth and heavens. The plans in His heart are wisdom. To know His heart—is wisdom to us.

To obtain wisdom, we must turn towards Him, humble ourselves, and seek Him with all of our heart, mind and strength. Wisdom is like walking in the light. The Spirit shines light the wisdom of God, personified as a woman in the book of Proverbs.

Even though, we don't admit it, our hearts are already known to God. For, He is God, and He knows everything. When we are willing to open them to Him, we can have a mutual flow heart to heart with our Creator. For, when we open our heart to Him, then He will open His to us. Have we have moved the heart of God?

A Sky Bridge

There is a sky bridge between the spirit of wisdom and the spirit of understanding—between knowing the mind of God and understanding it.

When I was studying for my degree in Nursing, I took Statistics as a subject. My final grade was an A. I knew the subject, but did not understand it! I could recite enough to pass the exams—but have no working knowledge of how it relates to the field of Nursing.

In the spiritual kingdom we need a bridge to knowing and understanding, otherwise we become stupidly smart—we know a lot about the subject, but do not have the tools to implement it.

> Knowledge puffeth up, but charity edifieth. And if any man think that he knoweth any thing, he knoweth nothing yet as he ought to know. But if any man love God, the same is known of him. *I Corinthians 8.1b-3* **Christian New Testament**

The Spirit of Understanding is to know why God does things a certain way because there is an understanding of His way of thinking.

Let me give an example—If someone hands my husband a cat, he will pet it for a while, then put it down and go outside. I know that he is allergic to cats. He doesn't tell others, but attempts to compensate for his behavior by being kind in holding their cat, then needing to breathe by going outside.

This may seem like a silly analogy to explaining the Spirit of Understanding as it relates to God, but there is a correlation. If we know God as a personal being, then we will understand Him. Not that we could ever understand God, but we can get an idea by becoming familiar with Holy Books and interactive prayer with Him. Then, like the analogy of my husband, if we understand Him we will pray better. For, certainly we wouldn't pray for our brother to be cursed if we know that God desires to bring blessing.

What I have come to realize is there is a bridge between the house of Wisdom and the house Understanding within the Kingdom of God. It is called *inspiration.* It provides the link between the two houses making a way to walk from one to the other.

For example—the dream which I just related about the young Hindu lady who saw the face of one God in the face of another—She didn't understand the dream before she brought it to me, so she didn't know how to get to the answer which was to receive power to help others be healed and comforted.

I asked God for the answer in prayer and listened to His voice sent by the Spirits of Wisdom and Understanding accompanied by the Spirit of Presence and was given **insight** into the answer. The *insight* is the bridge which enabled her to pass over from *knowing* the dream to *understanding* the dream. And, once she understood the dream, then she could walk into the answer of her question which brought others what they needed.

When I interpreted her dream, I felt that both dreams (taken together) were saying she did not need to *convert* to different faith to see a new face of God. She could see the face which she was looking for—within the faith which she now had.

Recognize that I am not against converting to another faith, because I am Catholic, and there is a reason for that, but, at this point I have taken my own beliefs out of the equation and have been asked to interpret a dream—and it's not my dream, but hers.

The dream of the young Hindu lady was about trusting God to show which ever face He desired to whomever He desired. We have a tendency to assume that the face which we see the most is the *best* one.

It doesn't seem right to assume the *Spirit of Inspiration* is a separate entity, yet at the same time, it becomes alive when we get there because, out of all of the Holy Books which I have studied, it is one of the most important aspects of the book.

> *Paul who wrote many of books of the Christian New Testament prays for the congregation which he sends letters to frequently* that they—may have a Spirit of Wisdom and Inspiration which will enable them to know God better because then, they will see things with the eyes of their heart instead of their physical eyes. *Ephesians 1.17-20* **Christian New Testament**

I believe that is the key—for us to begin to see things with spiritual eyes rather than physical eyes, or mental eyes. We can look at circumstances and go along the river of life bumping around rocks and through currents hoping our boat won't flip over we will arrive at a destination—or we can take many classes and achieve great learning of religious books so that our mind is quick and alert. We can fast and be disciplined in exercise of our faith—but to see life with spiritual eyes, we need something which we do not have—*spiritual insight*. Without the Spirit of Inspiration we cannot connect the Wisdom of God with understanding of spiritual principles.

There is a promise given in the Great Book (Old Testament) that says we will receive inspiration if we wait for it. God wants for us to understand what He means when He gives a message. The Spirit of Inspiration as it connects with the Wisdom of God and the Understanding of God brings the answer to our questions.

> Write down the revelation and make it plain on tablets so that a herald may run with it. For the revelation awaits an appointed time; it speaks of the end and will not prove false. Though it linger, wait for it; it will certainly come and will not delay. *Habakkuk 2.3* **Tanakh**

The author of the Qur'aan also recognized the importance as he penned this verse.

> It is Inspiration which provides guidance and assurance of the hereafter. *Surah 2.4* **Qur'aan**

Inspiration is in the third sentence in the introduction to the **Book of Mormon.** The ability to know and understand spiritual guidance which comes from God is important to their faith. The Spirit of Counsel gives direction. The Spirit of Might provides power. With this combination there is direction with ability to carry through by the release of His power.

The Spirit of Knowledge provides information about who God is. When we seek evidence of God, we learn about His many Beautiful Names and how they affect our lives. This Spirit explains who He is. In essence, we ask Him to explain Himself. Do you ever wonder why someone does something a certain way? You can wonder—or you can ask.

I use simple analogies, but feel many work too hard to understand spiritual principles.

For instance, I can wonder why my husband takes a shower after he mows the grass, or I can ask. If I ask he will tell me, "I need to wash off the pollens that get kicked up by the mower so I do not have an allergy attack."

Many times we wonder how God feels about something going on in our lives or in the world. We wonder, yet neglect to ask Him. Why?

Many ask, but fail to understand the answer as in the dream I recently mentioned. God rarely speaks to us in an audio voice. The spirit of God has innumerable ways He communicates. There are dreams, visions, impressions, and Nature to name a few. We are dull to assume He cannot answer our questions. The X-factor is our ability to understand the answer. This is where the bridge called *insight* come in.

Consider coming across a distressed person. When you ask him what is wrong, he speaks in a language you do not understand. Does it mean he didn't try to communicate? Because we do not recognize or understand when God is attempting to communicate does not mean He isn't. The problem isn't with Him, but us.

> But the natural [unbelieving] man does not accept the things [the teachings and revelations] of the Spirit of God, for they are foolishness [absurd and illogical] to him; and he is incapable of understanding them, because they are spiritually discerned and appreciated, [and he is unqualified to judge spiritual matters]. *I Corinthians 2.14* ***New Testament Amplified Version***

Again, insight (inspiration) is the bridge between the house of Wisdom and the house Understanding within the Kingdom of God. I know something; but do I understand it? Linking the two makes a bridge enabling us to walk from one to the other. We cannot think to understand the spiritual kingdom using physical elements. It doesn't work. We cannot drag God into our zone. How about we do to His?

Spirit of God

God is not physical, but spiritual and dwells in a holy place while we dwell with our feet planted on the earth. We are surrounded by sin and degeneration, so how do we think to understand His ways except that He reveals them to us?

Ah, but He does—*spirit to spirit.* We are created mind, body and spirit. The mind permits us to calculate decisions. The body enables us to voice our opinion. The spirit enables us to communicate on a higher level, interact with that which is spiritual, and be eternal.

> Then God said, "Let us make mankind in our image, in our likeness, so that they may rule over the fish in the sea and the birds in the sky, over the livestock and all the wild animals,[a] and over all the creatures that move along the ground."
>
> So God created mankind in his own image, in the image of God he created them; male and female he created them.
>
> God blessed them and said to them, "Be fruitful and increase in number; fill the earth and subdue it. Rule over the fish in the sea and the birds in the sky and over every living creature that moves on the ground." *Genesis 1.26-28* **Tanakh**

Indeed we are unique from all other living creatures because we are created in the image of God. Are we God? No. May we never forget that He is the One with the power to give breath and take it away.

When I was a young nurse starting out working in the ICU, I thought that if someone had a pacemaker and was on a respirator, he could live forever. I reasoned that the breathing machine kept his lungs going while the pacemaker kept the heart beating, so why would he die?

Some lived longer than others. So, I reasoned, perhaps *their* will-to-live kept them alive. I changed my opinion when my 48-year-old mother, who had everything to live for and was a very spiritual person, died. No machines or a tenacious will-to-live could keep her alive.

A Muslim cardiologist once told me, "My theory is that we all have been given a heart that has a specific amount of beats. When those beats are done, then it stops. In essence we are *timed-out.*"

More accurately, probably, God owns the breath. He gives and He takes it away.

Are we without options? I don't think so. I have seen otherwise.

For fifteen years I worked in the Cardiac ICU in a renowned Heart Hospital in Las Vegas. My job was to recover the patients after open heart surgery. Dr. Chowdry (who I mention in the front of the book) performed open heart surgery on a lady and I was selected to become her recovery nurse.

She arrived with a swarm of medical staff bustling around the bed. They parked the bed in the empty room quickly and handed me four units of blood with the understanding that I should infuse them, "Right now because she was bleeding and they could not stop it!"

Several nurses joined me and we frantically hung all of the drips and placed the lady on a respirator (as was protocol.)

I looked up at the machines which monitored her vital signs and saw they were still flat so I yelled to the OR Staff, "Hey get back here. You forgot to hook her up to the monitors!"

Only pausing his step briefly, the OR Tech responded, "We did. She doesn't have any vital signs."

Her husband arrived at the bedside right then and began yelling at Dr. Chowdry—who had followed the patient out of the OR, "I leave my wife alive in the morning and you give her back to me dead! How can you do this?"

Dr. Chowdry wasn't very good at diffusing anger, so they got into a loud argument at the foot of the bed. There were supplies flying all over the room, a floundering ICU patient and an angry husband yelling at the Cardiac Surgeon, so I suggested the husband wait in the waiting room.

He went to the waiting room, and to my surprise, Dr. Chowdry sat quietly outside the ICU room. Usually the surgeons retreat to get cleaned up. He did not; but stayed.

As I busily tended to the ICU drips I prayed fervently for the lady laying listlessly in the bed before me. Several nurses and a respiratory therapist ran in to the room and began praying as well. They had to return to their work, so they left shortly. I stayed.

The monitors stayed flat without a sign of life. When patients have heart surgery their body is cooled, so sometimes they take a while to come back; so I was not panicked at this time—just prayerful.

Then I saw her spirit begin to leave her body. I said, "Spirit I command you back into the her body."

When I did that, all of a sudden, the machines which indicate 'life' came alive! She had vital signs! After a minute or so, her eyelids began to flutter open.

I called to Dr. Chowdry who was sitting outside the room, "Dr. Chowdry, she has vital signs."

He hurried into the room to confirm it was true. He said, "How did this happen?"

So, I told him, "I saw her spirit try to leave her body, so I commanded it back into her body. Then she began to show signs of life."

His response was amusing. He inquired, "What exactly does that look like?"

I replied, "Oh, Dr. Chowdry. You cannot know what that looks like unless you are willing to go there. If you ask God to show you spiritual things, then you must be willing to see not only the positive but the negative spiritual things because you can't pick and chose. If you want your spiritual eyes to be opened, then they will be opened to see both."

The lady survived and went home after a few days of recovery.

––––––––––––––

I give this example to show definitively we are divided into parts. Not often do we seem them separate, but we may. What I said to Dr. Chowdry is true; if you want to see the things of the spiritual world, you can ask. But, you cannot pick and choose between seeing only the *nice* things because you have no control over that world. Normally, we live in a default world of only understanding what is in front of our eyes. Understanding of the things of the spirit is ours if we ask the source of all understanding—God.

> But the natural [unbelieving] man does not accept the things [the teachings and revelations] of the Spirit of God, for they are foolishness [absurd and illogical] to him; and he is incapable of understanding them, because they are spiritually discerned and appreciated, [and he is unqualified to judge spiritual matters] I Corinthians 2.14 *Christian New Testament AMP*

The idea of us being transported into a spiritual place of understanding things of the spiritual world is not new. Since the creation of man, the opportunity to comprehend spiritual things has been around. We just don't know how to get there. Again—we need the tools to be able to cross over into an unseen world. We need to be in a place where we can receive messages. However, we cannot see God, because He is a Spirit.

Yet, there is a bridge wherein our spirit can to communicate with His Spirit through a special which He provided when we were created by His power and authority. It is not new as indicated by the verse below from Genesis.

> The earth was formless and void or a waste and emptiness, and darkness was upon the face of the deep [primeval ocean that covered the unformed earth]. The Spirit of God was moving (hovering, brooding) over the face of the waters. Genesis 1.2 *Tanakh*

God created humans and instilled within them the ability to recognize His divine nature. It is like we are created as computer having a terminal where a wire is able to fit. The Spirit of God [the Holy Spirit] brings understanding of God.

> God {Allah} is the One who reveals the interpretation of spiritual things. "Thus will your Lord choose you and teach you the interpretation of stories (and events) and perfect His favor to you and to the posterity of Jacob – even as He perfected it to your fathers Abraham and Isaac aforetime? For Allah is full of knowledge and wisdom." *Surah 2.6 **Qur'aan***

The Holy Spirit of God is the interpreter making clear the works of God. In essence, He explains Himself through the spiritual aspect of His person.

Divine Inspiration

Divine inspiration comes
when we open our soul to the light.
Remember, the light doesn't come from us
because we aren't divine

He Pushes His Purpose

Meditation Words: *We have to see the purpose before we can see the presence. He pushes you into the presence by direction.*

Understanding of the words: We cannot get into the presence of God without His direction. God is Holy and we are pretty far from it. But, He provided hope. The Spirit of God has been working before we were born to coax us toward Him. God has always purposed to be friends with us. We could never drag Him onto our side of the tracks because of our sinfulness, but in His love for us, He provided a way to lift us to His side—His holy side.

The purposes of God are built on His word. We can stand firm on His word; His promises. It is possible to tap into the mind of God because of His interpreter, the Holy Spirit. He helps to understand God's ways. He explains the mysteries. Then, to top it off, He provides power to bring those plans into fulfillment. He unites His purpose with His plans into fulfillment according to His power flowing through us as we open our heart up to Him.

God has an intended purpose for each of us. He has planned for us to have a place within the building of the Kingdom, no matter which faith we are involved in—or apart from. If we allow, His mission will thread through our ministry, our teaching, and our way of life. Our ways will be His ways, not our own. When God has a purpose to fulfill, He will call on someone who will do it. He has given us the Spirit of Wisdom to help direct into the building of His Kingdom. When we do not seek His counsel, then our plans fail. But, when we seek His purposes, He will rescue us His way, His direction. He won't drop us there, but will continue to lead through the rescue. His voice is alive—it is active. His word flows.

We can tap into receiving direction from Him any time. He looks for willing hearts open to receive.

Nehemiah 8.4, Job 17.11, 33.17, Proverbs 15.22, 20.18, Isaiah 14.24-27, 46.11, **Tanakh,** *II Corinthians 1.17, 9.11, Ephesians 1.9, 3.11, 2 Timothy 1.9, 3.10.* **Christian New Testament**

Contemplation of Beyond

Contemplation of beyond starts now.

For we have become a door to the future when we insert

the key into the slot of the door of the house

He has left us the deed to.

Praying the Plans of God

The wisdom of God is incorporated within His plan. He has made plans for the building of His Kingdom. There are plans for how the Kingdom of God on earth is to be raised up to become His desire.

As servants of God, become the pillars of the building process just like pillars of a building. What does this mean? We are the ones to hold the roof up over the heads of those who need protection from the weather of life. The only way we can become strong enough to uphold the Kingdom principles is to call upon God's strength.

If we are to be a pillar, how do we know where are we supposed to stand? We need to ask Him. He is the architect, the builder, and the contractor.

Wisdom provides what is needed to roll out the plans of God. The difference in His plans and our plans is that He has all the ability to fulfill them to completion. He has the supplies. He backs His word. When He says something, it is as good as done. It is through His word that the world was created.

Prayer activates the plans of God. When we know the plans of God, we can pray into them. Prayer connects the heart of God to the power. It is as if God speaks His plans into being when we pray. It is one of the great mysteries. Why would God set up a system that He needs us to pray His will into being? Indeed, this is the truth in action through prayer. When we pray, His wisdom flows through us bringing victory.

Through wisdom the house is built, and through understanding it is established. When we hear God's voice, we need to understand it before we can obey it. *Through knowledge all the rooms of God are filled with rare and beautiful treasures.*

> By wisdom a house is built, and through understanding it is established; through knowledge its rooms are filled with rare and beautiful treasures. Proverbs 24.3,4 ***Tanakh***

> Say the Holy Spirit has brought the inspiration from your Lord in Truth, in order to strengthen those who believe, and as a guide and glad tidings to Muslims. *Surah 16.102* ***Qur'aan***

Mother Wisdom's Kitchen

When we cook in the kitchen of Mother Wisdom, we don't set our own timer. We need to carefully read the directions. For, the things to be adequately done in her kitchen, let her set the timer, the temperature, and the temperament. A cake is not good well done. It needs to be done well, carefully monitored in a controlled environment. Don't gripe if there is a cool down time after you finish a great project. The cake needs to cool. Chill out. Take a break. It is God's cake.

Who owns the stuff in the kitchen of the Spirit of Wisdom? God. Why do we think we can steal His time, money and energy to expend it for our own glory?

Time spent *not* doing His project, resources thrown aside, old dreams and visions never interpreted, or prayers with wrong motives resulting in having the wrong stuff at the wrong time. If people ask of us; we need to ask God for direction. Not all of the people who ask for our help need our help. Perhaps, they need God's help directly, instead. By us helping, we get in the way of God's voice to them.

Knowledge of God

Once the foundation is established through Wisdom, then God can begin to build the house. Knowledge helps to learn who God is.

We need to set ourselves to learn the scriptures. The more scripture that we know, the greater understanding we will have of His principles. He can teach us quicker if we have a knowledge base. God continually calls scriptures to my mind and teaches me principles related to His wisdom, understanding and inspiration. There is an interrelationship between the 7 Spirits of God that in inseparable.

The knowledge of God did not end with what was already written down. We are shallow if we think that any *one Holy* book contains all of the knowledge of who God is. The copy of the Qur'aan which I am referring to as I write this book recounts over and over making reference to things which are written in what is considered the *Old Testament* as well as *Christian writings* related to the teachings of Jesus.

The introduction to the Book of Mormon states, "This book is comparable to the *Bible*, yet it does not usurp the authority of that book as if it could be replaced."

The account of the book of Mormon proposes that it was written because Moroni was given a commandment by the spirit of prophecy and inspiration. *Introduction **Book of Mormon***

> Again, the Qur'aan states that He is the Lord of the Throne of authority: by His command He sends the spirit of inspiration to any of His servants He pleases, that it may warn men of the Day of Mutual Meeting. *Surah 40.15 **Qur'aan.***

As we seek Him, He will continue to speak to our heart through which ever channels we are willing to open up to His voice. He desires for us to know Him, so He continues to share more and more of Himself with us. Knowledge of God provides the framework for His voice to speak into.

Understanding God

If we want understanding it will cost. It doesn't come free. When we understand God we know, not merely who He is, but what He likes. When we love someone, we don't know what he or she *likes* until we learn about him.

Here is a correlation: I have several friends that read tabloid magazines. When I hear them talk about movie stars, it is as if they know the star that is in the magazine. They do not know these stars personally, but know all about them as if they were personal friends.

Our relationship with God is this way. We can know all about Him without knowing Him. We can read His Holy Books and learn about His ways, but until we step into understanding Him as in a personal relationship, then we don't really know Him.

And the question one might ask is, "Are we too bold to assume to have a *friendly* type of relationship with God Almighty?"

Certainly we are not worthy, and not, by any means equal to Him so that we could possibly see eye to eye as if we were relating to one of our friends over coffee.

After attending several types of religious environments (Baptist Church, Synagogue, Temple, Mosque, Catholic Church) I have noticed that one huge differentiation is the honor and reverence which they use when addressing God (Allah.)

My husband, Paul, was brought up being trained as an altar boy within the Catholic Church. Within this structure of faith, they extend their reverence to God in several ways. For example, there is always water placed near the door which is used for those who enter into the sanctuary to bless themselves. As the parishioners come into the building, they dip their finger tips into the water and make a sign (using their arm) which indicates that they wish to obtain a blessing from entering the building. (At least that's the way I understand it. Perhaps many Catholics will have a more *spiritual* version, but this will work for the sake of my example within the context of this book.)

A few years ago, I visited some relatives who were Baptist. Somehow as the night progressed, the conversation drifted to customs related to Catholics. A comment was made, "Catholics need a spittoon at the door of their church."

Well, you can imagine that there was nearly a fist fight within the family. And, why was that? It was because the individual who spoke these things was unaware of reason behind the custom. *I sincerely hope that he did not learn this within the Church where he attends because I can't image someone encouraging that thinking.*

To someone who is unknowing, it looks like a bowl that has some water in it and everybody is dipping their hand into it as they walk by. When you think about it, without any insight, it really does look funny.

But, to those who have been reared within that faith, the dipping of the finger tips means that he or she is willing to be put into a place of paying attention to spiritual things. He sets behind the things on the outside (of the building) and sets his gaze on what God might want to teach him (or her) this day.

I saw the same type of thing happen when I attended a Mosque along with a friend as I studied the faith in preparation to writing this book. Wanting to show honor to their faith and recognizing that I had not been raised to understand their customs, I carefully studied for several months obtaining books from my Muslim friends and going to them with questions. Then, I joined them in the Ramadan fast so that I could help to understand the need for purity which is taught within their faith. As my (Muslim) friends watched me closely, they saw that, indeed, I fasted and studied hard. I proved to them that I was serious, not curious and not attempting to infiltrate the faith to tear it down. At the close of the fast, I requested to be invited to the Mosque to pray.

Well, another of my friends (who is not Muslim) asked, at the last moment to come along. I believe that her motivation was *curiosity* more than anything. While I was making sure that I fulfilled my *pillars of the faith* she was trying to figure out where to park her shoes before entering the sanctuary.

Everything seemed to go OK until an old lady spotted my friend. I am pretty sure that we were the only Anglo-Saxon white women there, so it was easy to pick us out in the crowd. Well, this lady came right up to us and gave us the look over from top to bottom, then began yelling at my friend because she was *guilty* of chewing gum. I mean this lady went ballistic!

Well, the women *who had invited us* who were with us (the women are separated from the men) jumped in to protect her and an argument began which escalated out of proportions. Being the friend that I am, I backed slowly out of the picture and held up the wall. It took five female Muslim doctors to pull off one old lady kicking and screaming at my friend.

You see, she pegged the gum…but what the real problem was that she was wearing a plaid suit and red lipstick. So, the old woman was screaming, "She dishonors God by coming into our place of worship this way."

The Muslim doctors retaliated with, "She and her friend are studying our faith and we have invited them in to see it."

But the angry woman spat back these words, "Then, if you invited them in, it was your responsibility to teach them what is proper and what is not proper. None of you belong in this house, either, because you don't know what is proper within this place."

So, I ask: Who is right?

All of them are right within their context. And, that is what we must believe in order to have peace between faiths. We don't need to convert to their faith and we don't need to understand, but we need to respect the way in which they worship. It shows our honor of God when we are able to enter into another place of *faith* and show respect within their structure while we worship God the way we know how.

You see, the true worship of God isn't in action, but in heart. One of the things I learned about the Muslim faith is that they move their body in a specific way in attempt to remind themselves of the way they need to be faithful to God. How amazing is that? During their worship they assume different postures. The postures are symbolizing a mental response to God in *all ways of life*.

I attend the Jewish Messianic Synagogue in Las Vegas as often as I can. They excel in reverence during their worship service. They have a point during the service where they open the Scriptures. They keep the Scriptures on a *scroll* in this special cupboard. As they open the cupboard and remove the scroll there is a ceremony. Then, the scroll is paraded around the entire sanctuary while a dance is played. Everyone is encouraged to reach out touching the scroll with the hem of their garment or their interpretation of the Scriptures (Hand held Bibles) and bring back a kiss. They show an open demonstration of *love for the Scriptures*.

And not to be found bashing the Baptists, let me say that they excel in sharing their faith with others. They have wonderful programs for their small children. If someone grew up Baptist, then he or she knows the keys to salvation, Bible Stories and song after song because they are very good at teaching the youngsters. The Baptists are the ones who buy buses and run them into rural areas to pick up youngsters whose parents won't bring them to Church because they have a special heart for the children.

Baptists are givers as well. They make sure nobody goes home hungry on Sunday. Many Churches have oodles of food for all on Sunday.

Back to the original question, "Is it OK to be friends with God?"

He says so…and don't forget Moses, Abraham, and Jacob. They were all friends of God. It says that Moses was a friend of God as one would have a friend face to face. Certainly if Moses could be friends with God, then it must be OK.

> And the LORD spake unto Moses face to face, as a man speaketh unto his friend. And he turned again into the camp... Exodus 33.11 ***Tanakh***

Yet, this friendship isn't like buddy, buddy because it was with God. It is a spiritual relationship, not a physical relationship. Some of the people which I have met who have the closest relationship with God are those who never *talk* with Him. You see, God doesn't need words. He isn't German or Russian, or English, or American. He is God and He responds to our spirit. Many times individuals who are *Churched up* or

Very Religious are the ones who are the furthest from God because their religious teaching of who God *should be* gets in the way of allowing Him to tell them who He really is.

Some years back when I worked in the ICU as a nurse there was an old man on a ventilator who had no family visiting him. He was all alone day after day on a breathing machine with no hope of coming off the machine to breathe on his own. In this state, you needed to be talking to make a decision to *pull the plug*. He couldn't speak because he was on the ventilator, so he was in a bad place. One day I noticed some visitors came, so I went into the room and asked them if they felt close enough to him to be able to make a decision for him to come off the ventilator and possibly die? They decided, because he was their father's best friend, they were OK with the decision. They signed the papers and, after a short time departed.

Even with the paperwork in place, the old man did not want to die. So, I asked him if he would like me to pray with him a final prayer. He nodded and I said, "I will pray for you with my voice and you pray with your heart. I know God will hear your heart before He hears my voice."

I prayed with him a final prayer and he was at peace to be removed from the ventilator and die in peace. He died with a smile on his face a couple of days later.

***

Being a friend of God is easiest for those who are honest with Him, yet approach Him with reverence and honor recognizing His Holiness exceeds theirs. You see, if you know nothing about Scriptures, it is possible to be friends with God. But, the problem is that, if you know nothing of Scriptures, then you are unaware of how others have successfully had relationships with Him and worshiped Him.

If you don't have anything to base your knowledge on except hearing His voice, then you have nothing to compare the voice which you hear with. And, if you have nothing to compare the voice with, you may be hearing the voice of another spirit believing that it is God's voice when it is not.

And, haven't we heard stories of how the *voice* told someone to kill their loved ones and he thought it was God telling him to do it, so he did? How preposterous to think that God would tell someone to kill his loved ones! To you and I it seems silly because we know that God wouldn't say such a thing. And, how do we know that? The Scriptures teach otherwise.

Proverbs, Ecclesiastes, Job, **Tanakh,** *John,* **Christian New Testament** *Surah 55.1-2* **Qur'aan.**

The Spirit of Counsel

One of the Seven Spirits of God.

God is as interested in our plans, as well as in the outcome of them. When we exclude Him from them, He knows. His ears and eyes are always upon His servants, no matter whether we are doing what He wants us to or following our own path. Our plans provide the seed for what we intend to do, so you can bet He is interested.

Maybe we listen to friend's advice, the television, or our own experience for direction. When we devise a plan of action that is not taken from consulting God, then we have a *seed* for sin. When we follow that plan, there will be problems—further sins. Sin has birthed sin.

If we stop sin at the seed rather than after it has grown a plant, then we will be saved from a lot of hurt. The seed of sin is a plan that is not from God, but from somewhere else.

For example, maybe someone has done us wrong, so we plan retaliation to that person who has hurt us. When we retaliate, he responds. We have prompted him to sin. Sin has conceived and brought forth another sin. Our seed, our plan, has yielded fruit after its kind.

Let's be more *spiritual* about it. Suppose we decide to become a missionary to the American Indians. We sell our home and move the family to the reservation. We can't speak the language and do not have a gift of evangelism, so, we become frustrated. Our anger is transferred to our family and we start to have disputes. There is no money because God does not promise to provide for plans that are outside of His.

Discouraged and despaired, we return to our old way of life. The sin of planning without God's ideas has conceived and brought forth more sins and grown a tree that we planted with our own seeds. When we plant a tree, we have no ability to tend it because we do not have the power of provision.

The Spirit of God has been given to provide us with counsel. When our spirit bears witness with the Spirit of God, we receive His counsel into our heart. The Holy Spirit drops things into our heart, not our mind. Our mind has to be open to receive the things of God from our heart for these ideas to become real to us.

We have no reason to feel like we are stumbling around in the dark with regard to direction in our lives from God. When we call to Him, He offers advice from so many directions, that our way will be lit up ahead of us like a trail of fluorescent fish along the shore line. God doesn't mind giving confirmation when we are unsure which way to go. He likes to direct us. He guides us with His eye upon us.

> I will instruct you and teach you in the way you should go; I will guide you with My eye. Psalm 32.8 *Tanakh*

When God directs us, He gives us the opportunity to talk with Him about the plans. He is not like a military officer who commands His soldiers and then goes back to the central office leaving the soldiers to fight alone. The Lord desires to sit down with us and talk over the plans before He helps us to enact them. We need to take time to sit with Him and listen to His counsel. He wants to listen to us as well. He desires our lives to become a conversation with Him.

To get direction from God into our lives, there is an interaction between the scriptures and hearing the Voice of God into our lives for today. The scriptures teach about who God is and His ways; His character. When we study the scriptures, we come to know what God likes and doesn't like, so when we are presented with a decision, we have an idea of which one He will select based on His selections of the past.

Many listen to God through the scriptures as they read them on a daily basis. On the other hand, there are those who are religious yet do not read the scriptures on a daily basis. These ones *ask* Him for direction. He gives them prompting within their spirit through a gentle voice. They follow the *voice* or *their gut* for direction, rather than the scriptures. Who is right? Both.

It is like a bowling alley. We want to keep our ball out of the gutter. When small children bowl, they have these blow up things that they put in the gutter to keep the ball from going into it. God has provided us with blow ups to keep us out of the gutter. One side is the scriptures and the other side is the Spirit of Counsel.

When we are familiar with the scriptures, it is like knowing someone. I like the example of tabloids filled with personal stores of movie stars.

If someone gets to know a movie star through following their life by reading tabloids for years, do they know him or her? No. They know all about the star, but do not know him because they do not have a personal relationship with him.

This is similar to knowing God (because you talk Him) or reading the history of how He related to others through time in scriptures. The holy books give insight into the character and mind of the Creator. Talking with Him; learning to communicate spirit to Spirit brings a deeper level of a relationship—it becomes personal.

Some religions attempt to wall-off insight into who God is by prohibiting believers from reading other books. Do you think *all* of the information about God is contained in a single book? That is absurd. Can you contain all of the knowledge on you in a book? No.

God is the creator of the ever-expanding universe, so do not be tricked into thinking all of the knowledge of Him is given in any book. He transcends everything.

Consider the Spirit of Counsel who knows the heart of God. Come to Him for answers.

Psalms 13, 33,73,107,119, Proverbs 1,8,11,15,19,21, Isaiah ,8,11,19, 22, 29, 46, Job 12.13, 38.2, 42.3, **Tanakh,** *Romans 11.34, I Corinthians 4.5, Hebrews 6.17.* **Christian New Testament.**

The Manifold Presence of God; Kingdom Food

Ho, every one that thirsteth, come ye to the waters, and he that hath no money; come ye, buy, and eat; yea, come, buy wine and milk without money and without price. Wherefore do ye spend money for that which is not bread? and your labour for that which satisfieth not? hearken diligently unto me, and eat ye that which is good, and let your soul delight itself in fatness. Incline your ear, and come unto me: hear, and your soul shall live; and I will make an everlasting covenant with you, even the sure mercies of David. Isaiah 55.1-3 *Tanakh*

Come to His Banquet Table

Coming to God's banquet table is like being invited out to dinner with someone you love. When we come to His restaurant, we seek Him, He comes to the table. This is the water. When we start to drink from His presence, this is the milk. Then we begin to have conversation with one another.

This is the bread. He begins to tell us what His plans are for His Kingdom and we start to enter into those plans. We see how we fit into His plans as well. Then we have gotten to the meat. We have met Him at His goals. After a while, He lights the candles and pours the wine.

We have reached a point in our relationship when we meet not to ask for things, not to be given instructions, not to have a planning meeting; but to just enjoy one another's company. This is the wine. This is finding the delight in His presence because we are in love with Him and He is in love with us.

When we think there can be nothing greater, double joy comes to us when we pull up a chair for someone else. The joy of God flows through our life as the anointing given to us is shared with someone else in the presence of the Spirit.

Water

It is possible to pray for a desire to thirst to know God. The answer arrive as we are given water first. When our soul has been without a relationship with God, then we are *dry*, starved, and barren like a desert without water. As we pray and the Holy Spirit comes to us, it feels like immersion of cool water bringing satiation to our soul.

We are like a cup waiting to be filled. In order for us to be filled, we must be empty of ourselves. We must let go of all the things we are hanging onto which separate and come between us and God. This empties our cup and makes it ready to be filled with the cool water of the Holy Spirit.

Often, we come up with our own words that help us to deal with our separation from God. We think up excuses for our sin and blame God for being distant from us. Our words only *swirl* around—they don't bring real hope to our lost soul. At times we consult others about happiness and hope. Then, we follow their advice. This is as drinking *stolen* water. We are not be satiated. Counselors cannot fill a dry soul. They may pad our agony and dull the pain with chemicals and therapy, but true hope for a dry soul only comes from God. He created us with a place in our being which can only be accommodated by His Spirit communing with ours. Ask and let Him flood your soul.

Job 21:24, Psalms 74:13, Proverbs 5:15, Song of Solomon 4:11, Isaiah 28:9-17, 37:25, 55:1, Amos 8:11, ***Tanakh.*** John 4. ***Christian New Testament*** 1 Nephi 17.45 ***The Book of Mormon*** Surah 31.12 ***Qur'aan*** Book of Wisdom 1.1 ***The Wisdom books of the Old Testament in the Catholic Bible.***

Milk

Milk comes after the birth of the baby, to provide nourishment enabling growth. Milk is the first food that comes from the mother to the infant.

Initially when we come to God with a dry soul, He provides water. After a while, we, like newborns given milk, should look for sustenance in our relationship with Him—learning how to merge our spirit with His. We must learn how to *feed* off of Him—how to be nurtured by His words to our soul. The milk is the words of God to help us with life while we are on the earth before we enter into the presence of God himself.

We can be fed by others—they tell us where to read in Holy Books and offer principles of prayer. But, in order to grow—just like a baby should grow into a man, we must learn to seek God apart from other's direction. And, to follow the baby analogy, we should move on to *chewing*—or meditation on the things which are important to God.

Isaiah 2.35, 60, 66.9, **Tanakh,** *I Corinthians 3.2, 9.7, Hebrews 5.12, I Peter 2.2, I John 2.27,* **Christian New Testament**

Bread

The bread is the interactive *presence* of God. We give it to God, and He gives it to us. It is one of the only things shown in every Holy Book I have read, that men are called to give to God and He sends it back. It is a volley.

The Israelites were saved, delivered, and then given bread from heaven daily. The manna from heaven gave a picture of seeking spiritual subsistence with fulfillment coming from Him. There is no need to wait until we enter into our final resting place to be with God. He has opened an option to commune with our spirit now.

It is difficult to image, but written down over and over, that God hungers for us in a way that cannot be described. When He lost fellowship with man in the Garden of Eden, He immediately looked toward regaining that fellowship with us. He missed it because He wants to commune with us. Do you think God has emotions? Is He sad or happy? Does He have unfulfilled desires?

Some teach God is a distant being, stern setting His absolute will into being. And like gravity pulling a roller coaster, His will cannot be altered because of the magnitude of His power at work. I am not sure if these teachings are true, but I adhere the reader to look deeper into the character of God—written in these Holy Books and many others—and ask the question. Yell it to the Universe and see if the Universe doesn't respond.

Are we not created in the image of God? We are mind, body and spirit. This means we have a form with mental capacity as well as an option for spiritualness. We have emotions and will. Do you suppose we were created similar to Him? If we were, then He has emotions and desires. We can learn about someone or we can get to know him.

*Genesis 3.19, Malachi 1,2, **Tanakh**, Matthew 4.4, 15,16, John 6, I Corinthians 5.8. **Christian New Testament**, Alma 5.34 **The Book of Mormon***

Meat

The meat is that portion of the Spirit which comes to us when we linger in His presence. To receive the meat, we must have already drank the water and eaten the bread. We have come to God, seen our lives changed, learned to feed daily at His banquet table with His holy presence. The meat is where God MEETS us. His faithfulness meets our obedience.

There is a greater depth of commitment to this level of presence with God. When we get to the meat, then we have learned how to listen to Him. We listen to Him, now we need to do what He wants us to do.

His presence grows within and there is an interdependence that is beginning to build.   Our hands start to become His hands to work for His Kingdom.   They are hands that can be trusted to do His mission. Their goals become His goals, because they realize that He has the best goals in store.

The Christian New Testament refers to the prophet, Jesus calling his *meat* doing the will of God and finishing His work. The goal is to *meet* God an every turn to provide strength and guidance to complete the tasks at hand.

The meat takes time to prepare. It is the main course. We must use both hands so we can cut it up. This is the place that weeds out those who are half hearted. Obedience to the word through the provision of His grace.

Numbers 29.6, Job 34.3,12.1, Psalms 111.5,145, Malachi 3.10, **Tanakh.**

Wine

When we come thirsty to the table of God's presence, He will provide us with Himself. We only bring our willing heart, nothing else. All our works are like bringing dirty dishes to a clean table. God has supplied all we need there. To get to the wine, we first must seek His presence, then learn to drink from Him; His words to us. We learn how to incorporate the voice of God within our lives. The meat is where we learn obedience to what He tells us to do with the meat, there is a sense of mutual responsibility with God. We do what He tells us to do, and learn to claim His promises; then He does what we ask.

After, we have our fill of the meat, and then comes the wine. Wine is from pressed fruit. The meat produces the fruit in our lives as our gifts are demonstrated to those in need. When we continue to *press* in toward the presence of God, He brings us the wine. He sees our *passion* for Him and further *presses* us into service for Him.

The wine drinkers are those whom He gives the *hard jobs*. The wine is that which comes to us when we linger and enjoy the taste of Him. It is delight in Him. The joy wells up in our being and overflows into our life giving us a passion to know God more intimately. The high *spirits* come from the hand of the Lord who holds a cup of wine mixed with spices. The wine gladdens as the oil makes the face to shine, while the bread sustains. The Spirit brings His presence, the water, and turns it into an opportunity for us to continually abide with Him. He gave us the wine—the delight in the Holy Spirit.

We need to let Him touch us with His voice—with the kisses of His mouth because His love will touch us in a way that is more delightful than wine. He will sweep us off our feet and bring us into His Holy place.

*Palms 75.8, 104.15, Proverbs 9, Song of Solomon 1.2-4, Jeremiah 13.12, Hosea 9.4, Joel 3.18, Zechariah 10, Amos 9.13, **Tanakh.***

The Wall
Where Presence and Kingdom Meet

The dream: A Friend gives me a picture. I am standing on an upper wall around a city in front of a church structure. The wall is very tall— about 60 feet. I am at the very top of it looking forward balancing on the wall. I am surprised at how tall the wall is.

Then, he shows me another picture. It is the same city behind the wall, but in this picture it shows a second wall, that is lower. There is a woman standing on that wall too. She looks like she could be me, as well. In both pictures, the women are facing outward from the city, looking for something. They don't seem to notice that they are on top of a wall that is narrow.

Interpretation of the dream: In the dream, I am standing on a wall with an ancient city behind. It is the City of the Kingdom of God. Often, in the Scriptures, Israel (in the **Tanakh**) and the Church (in the **New Testament**) is regarded as a *wall* that God is building. The New Testament gives the analogy that believers are like *living stones* in the wall of the Kingdom of God. In essence, believers are part of the building process. We are part of the wall, itself.

When we learn our position within the Kingdom of God—the ancient City—then we will know where to stand. In the dream, I am standing on the wall. A wall can also be a structure built of stones. In the New Testament, the prophet Jesus refers to himself as a cornerstone and the capstone. And, so He is to the Christian faith.

Indeed, the Prophet Mohammed is a cornerstone for Islam. Many of the beliefs are built on principles that were given to him.

Joseph Smith is a cornerstone of the founding of the Church of the Latter-day Saints because many teachings are built from the principles he was given.

In each of these instances, the release to many is pivotal based on one person's teaching. The followers become as living stones in the wall which hold up the principles which are highly esteemed.

Those with no religion—even those who do not recognize a

cornerstone within their belief, stand on the wall of the Kingdom of God when they stand on the promises they feel that they have been given. They look forward for them to come to pass.

The correlation within the dream is that I was standing on two walls. On one wall, I understood *a lot* of teaching and was *taller* in my position. And, in the other picture, I was on a shorter wall, but still facing the same way. In both instances, I was focused on something that was coming over the hill and watching for it to happen.

Sometimes, we find ourselves standing on a low wall. In essence, we only have *a word or two* which we believe is from God, the Spirit, Allah, YHWH—or the Universe—and are looking toward the fulfillment of it. The message of the dream is that, no matter how small the promises are which you are standing on, you can look for His presence to meet His Kingdom. He comes home.

Just because we don't know a lot of scripture, we can still stand on whatever we know. All of the promises are true, so no matter which ones we claim, all of them are true. The X-factor is if we are hearing them correctly. That is a different subject to be covered in another book.

He has given us the power to pray in His Kingdom. He placed the keys to the Heavenly Kingdom in our hands. As members of this kingdom, we have a unique position between two kingdoms. We live in the world, yet we belong to the spiritual Kingdom of God. As we look to pray for needs, we ask for God's Kingdom to come.

We live in a *default* world. This Kingdom is run by *the prince of the power of the air—Satan.*

> Wherein in time past ye walked according to the course of this world, according to the prince of the power of the air, the spirit that now worketh in the children of disobedience... *Ephesians 2.2,3* **Christian New Testament**

> To Adam he said, "Because you listened to your wife and ate fruit from the tree about which I commanded you, 'You must not eat from it,'
> "Cursed is the ground because of you; through painful toil you will eat food from it all the days of your life. It will produce thorns and thistles for you, and you will eat the plants of the field. By the sweat of your brow you will eat your food until you return to the

ground, since from it you were taken; for dust you are and to dust you will return."

Adam named his wife Eve,because she would become the mother of all the living. The Lord God made garments of skin for Adam and his wife and clothed them. And the Lord God said, "The man has now become like one of us, knowing good and evil. He must not be allowed to reach out his hand and take also from the tree of life and eat, and live forever."

So the Lord God banished him from the Garden of Eden to work the ground from which he had been taken. 24 After he drove the man out, he placed on the east side[e] of the Garden of Eden cherubim and a flaming sword flashing back and forth to guard the way to the tree of life. Genesis 3.17-24 *Tanakh*

Without the intervention of God, there is pain, suffering, loss, and separation from Him. When He comes to help us, He brings relief from our problems; life and peace; joy and strength; hope for our despair.

We can ask for hope knowing that it will come because God promises to bring it to us when we ask. In essence, we stand upon the promises of God and look for salvation to come in our time of need.

We stand on this wall between the two kingdoms. It is here we will see the presence of God coming.

So this is what the Sovereign LORD says: "See, I lay a stone in Zion, a tested stone, a precious cornerstone for a sure foundation; the one who relies on it will never be stricken with panic. Isaiah 28.16 *Tanakh*

As you come to him, the living Stone—rejected by humans but chosen by God and precious to him—you also, like living stones, are being built into a spiritual house[a] to be a holy priesthood, offering spiritual sacrifices acceptable to God through Jesus Christ. For in Scripture it says: "See, I lay a stone in Zion, a chosen and precious cornerstone, and the one who trusts in him will never be put to shame. *I Peter 2.4,5 Christian New Testament*

God will come Himself to our rescue when we call out to Him because of His love for us. His presence comes with His will. We will be sturdy in our walk with God if our foundation is built on His promises while we look for His presence to come to our aid. It is like we are standing on a wall—the promises built upon one another one at a time.

We represent the Kingdom of God between two worlds. Our back is to the Kingdom of God. He backs us. Our front is to this world. When we pray from a position of standing on the Scriptures is like we are on top of a wall. From this position, we can see the presence of God coming to help those in need. When His presence comes, then His will is done and His Kingdom comes. They are inseparable.

The Spirit of Counsel

Meditation*: The presence of the Holy Spirit comes two ways.*

The Spirit of Counsel has brought direction through many holy voices in the past. In addition, God gives His Spirit on a daily basis to guide and direct. Both provide confirmation of one another. If the words are from God—whether or not you believe certain words are inspired or not—then the Spirit will confirm the truth of the message within to you.

> The Spirit himself bears witness with our spirit that we are children of God... Romans 8.16 ***Christian New Testament English Standard Version***

The Spirit of Counsel that brings us the Spirit of Truth. When we are aligned with God and listening with our spirit, He reveals what is right.

We do not need to convince others there is a *voice* that talks to us, telling us, because they will not understand. The Spirit of Truth can only be understood when it happens individually. He reveals Himself—as mentioned above. Someone who is not spiritual won't understand.

> But the natural [unbelieving] man does not accept the things [the teachings and revelations] of the Spirit of God, for they are foolishness [absurd and illogical] to him; and he is incapable of understanding them, because they are spiritually discerned and appreciated, [and he is unqualified to judge spiritual matters]I Corinthians 2.14 ***Christian New Testament Amplified Version***

Others may not be able to understand how it operates because they do not see God from the same perspective. Their relationship with God is theirs; ours is ours. It is similar to a relationship between two lovers. They develop a secret language based on things that have become special to each other. Things said take on special meaning because of the meanings that they have between themselves. God wants to become intimate with us and develop a secret language that is only understood by us and Him. He's that way.

> But the Advocate, the Holy Spirit, whom the Father will send in my name, will teach you all things and will remind you of everything I have said to you. John 14.26 ***Christian New Testament***

The Holy Spirit is the quiet voice that talks to our spirit. He is also the *voice* that verifies that the other *voice* is truly words from God. He is both. These are the two ways that the presence of God comes to us. The Spirit manifests His presence when His truth is proclaimed. The Word bears witness to itself when something is true.

I can tell when someone tells me something that they report as being from God. I feel a jolt of energy of the Spirit. It is like an electric shock wave pulses through my body. The individual doesn't need to spend time trying to convince me that the *message* he has been given is from the Spirit because God, Himself, sends His presence to verify the truth. That jolt is the Spirit in me bearing witness to the Holy Spirit message that is coming to me that it is true. When they meet, they *clap* just like a bolt of lightning that lights up the night. The presence of God meets the presence of God and there is a spiritual connection.

The Spirit of Might

Meditation: *God brings healing seven ways. Leading by God takes us His way, in His time. The day of atonement came three times. She came in the clouds.*

Healing Seven Ways

God heals by His seven spirits. When God shows up, all of Him comes. He does not just bring part of His presence. It's like when we show up for dinner at someone's house, we bring all of ourselves. We bring our body, our mind, our emotions, our problems—all of us.

The same provision is for us today. He provides His Holy Spirit to give us His presence daily, now. And, He will come again to bring us to Himself. He has provided three atonements. One past, one present and one in the future. All come in the clouds. The rescue of God comes in the clouds. We need to look up—seek heaven for the answers.

Flow to Others

The Spirit of Might is a flow Spirit. It is the flow of the power of God to others. God's Spirit comes to us two ways. When we ask Him to indwell us, the Holy Spirit comes to live inside of us. He makes His home within us. We become the temple of God by His Spirit that He has made to dwell within us.

When a brother is moved by the Spirit *by inspiration* to speak words, then the Spirit flows through him to us. When this happens, the Spirit comes to us from this brother or sister. The Spirit that dwells within us bears witness to the testimony that the words are from God. The two Spirits collide. They kiss—they clap. They laud God. Often, we get *goose bumps*.

The Spirit of Might flows through us when we proclaim the words of God to others. It is about the flow.

One of God's names is *Healer*. He calls Himself our deliverer and healer. The Spirit of Might is what is used to bring healing to those who are sick.

For I will restore health unto thee, and I will heal thee of thy wounds, saith the Lord; ... Jeremiah 30.17 ***Tanakh***

He brings His healing seven ways. Seven is His perfect number. When people are healed, they are not healed by our hand. No one has ever healed another except God alone. No doctor ever healed. They can train and perform procedures that help the body to heal. But, God alone brings healing.

In order for the Spirit of Might to flow we need to go to those in need—go to their house instead of trying to bring them to ours. We bring the presence of God to them. Then, we bring the essence of Him. We bring the complete present because all that He is, He has given to us. He makes Himself known to others through us.

God will bring perfect direction, teaching, counsel, power, and might. When we look at the person, we see their needs in the flesh. Often, we look at the temporal (shell) and ask for healing. We look with our physical eyes. God wants us to ask Him to open our spiritual eyes to see what needs to be healed. There is spiritual, physical and soul healing. Often, we disregard the other two areas.

When The Spirit opens our spiritual eyes, then He will provide a destination for us to pray toward. When He leads us in prayer, then we can follow that trail to lead to healing.

As a helper of another person, we need to remember to 'move out of the way so that the individual can get on the elevator.' Often we are standing in front of the elevator door and others cannot get on the elevator. The elevator is the vehicle that takes them up to the floor that they need to be on. It is what God wants to work with them to move them into His presence. If we are standing in-between their relationship with God, then it will impede their healing. God wants to speak to each of us individually. So, as you show the person the trail to their healing, then follow the trail back to the parking lot yourself. Back out of the room, and back out of their time with God. Let them talk to Him themselves, so it will become their healing.

One of the worst mistakes we can make is to allow someone to think that he needs to come to us for his message from God, or his healing.

He needs to seek it for himself; then it will become his testimony, not ours.

The Rescue of God Breaks Through

The rescue of God breaks through like He broke through the water and parted it for the Children of Israel to be led out of Egypt. This is faith.

When I hike in the mountains near Las Vegas, along the trail there you can look off in the distance and there are two mountain peaks. At a certain place on the trail, it looks as if they are one mountain and a person could stand in the saddle between the peaks. They are both sickle shaped and form a perfect U from this vantage point. I have prayed that God will help me to stand in that saddle between those peaks. The only thing between those two peaks is air.

The Holy Spirit is air. So we need to learn to stand on Him. But often, when we do what He wants us to do, we feel like we are out on a limb; on thin air. This is where God wants us to be; reliant on the Holy Spirit completely. So, several times, when I have prayed for something, I have prayed that God would put me between those mountains, in the place of faith, and that I would stand on air in the high place that He has planned for me. The places that God wants us to go are out of our reach and beyond our thinking. They are high places where our feet will never touch the ground. He wants us to depend on Him totally.

The riches of God released.

If the riches of God have been released why don't I have them?

> ...You do not have because you do not ask God. When you ask, you do not receive, because you ask with wrong motives, that you may spend what you get on your pleasures. James 4.2,3 Christian New Testament.

Do we have the wrong purposes when we ask, so He does not answer us? We need to get our purposes in line with Him, and then we will have all of the riches from heaven released. The right reason is for us to turn from the old way to His new way. We want to be the friend of God instead of the friend of the world. When we follow His mold in prayer for healing, it is like a key that fits into a big steel door on a penitentiary. We need to align ourselves with His mold. It is like a lock and key. When we get it right, the door will open with a rumble and a crash.

The Spirit of Might flows

The power of God is by the flow of the Holy Spirit. He does not give His Spirit by measure. If we have the Holy Spirit, we have all of Him. There is no such thing as *part of the gifts of God.* God does not give us part of Himself. If we have the Holy Spirit indwelling us, then at any time, He can raise up any spiritual gift that He wants.

The Might is the force—the press. It is the degree of pressure as from a valve. It is like a valve that releases the gas into the engine to make more power. The potential for the release is always there, but the valve needs to be opened to release it.

The valve needs to be turned sideways to open up for the might to be released. It is like we are the valve in the engine. We stand between the flow of the power (Holy Spirit) and the output to the engine to make the car run faster. The total power of God is available at any time, but it is released through our ministry; through us. It is as if we are the very hands of God reaching out to the world.

To release the Spirit of Might we need to become an obedient valve. We need to lay down. We need to flatten, like a lever that allows the gas to flow into the engine as it runs faster and faster. We need to turn our heart toward Him and open up at both ends. We need to open up to God, then open up to others. Whatever area of service He has put us in, He wants the Spirit of Might to flow through.

It is where the miracles happen. It is like when the wing is pulled in toward the F-14, it decreases the drag and the jet flies faster with more power. The power was always there, but had not been released because the flaps were in the way. We must become flat before God. Flatten ourselves. We are in the way of the release of the power—Might.

Mutual Oath

I swear to God.

He swears to me an oath: A bare affirmation

Chapter 4
Merging Souls

Merging Souls

We seek God with a piece of us we know little about; our soul. And He meets us from a place we know nothing about. It is not until our soul connects with His Soul that we can truly learn about either. They merge like a tributary coming into the Mississippi River. We are the trickling brook and He is the rushing water. Not until then do we realize we thought we were the rushing water. For it was all we knew. Up to then, we had only merged with other brooks. Ours was as fine a brook as theirs. In fact, we had waterfalls and beautiful pools where colorful rainbow trout spawn. And, some of the other ones we met were kind of muddy. But, then we met the River. There is only one River that flows into the sea. It is the water that moves you to a place where you can see things as they truly are, not as we would like them to be; but as they are. It is the place where absolute truth dwells. I guess that is what it is. We have merged with the Truth.

Holiness

Holiness is a process. We have a measure of holiness here on earth, and walk toward ultimate purity to be able to enter heaven and be with God at His place. At the end of the road to holiness God has His house. It is where the throne, the rainbows of color, and the singing for ever more are. There is no evil, no sin, no darkness, and no judgment, nothing vile in the presence of God. There is only laughing, beautiful singing, colors, and joy.

From His throne originates light, love and truth. The only way we can know holiness is to ask Him what it is, for there is nothing holy here on earth. The earth was tainted with sin when Adam and Eve were tricked by the serpent in the garden of Eden.

God has left us a coat with a lining called grace. It is like a thick winter coat that protects from the icy winter weather in Alaska. If we put on the coat that He left for us, then when He looks at us, He does not see who is under it, only the coat. We have the lining of His grace against our skin, so we will not be frozen from the frigid stare of the Lord as He looks on our sins. What we must do, is to borrow the coat so that we may enter into the holiness of the Lord. He does not mind, He left it here on the hanger for us on purpose, so we can use it any time we need to. It is like a winter cabin in the forest. He has left it stocked for us, if we should arrive when He is not home.

The problem is that the door to the cabin is locked. He has left the key hidden waiting for us to come along in our season. We cannot find it without some light. There is no light here on earth apart from what God provides. We need to light that torch to be able to see the way to the key. Ask for God to illumine the path to His holiness.

Through the Fire

We need to walk where Daniel walked into the furnace
and through the fire.
Held hand in hand by the only one able to keep
us from getting singed.
But we won't go.
The place of ultimate resting lies within.
Thee and thou
Me and you,
one surrounding love.

The Eye of the Tornado

Be His eyes.
We cut through the fog to see what He shows us.
The eyes of the storm.
The way is in the middle of the tornado.
In the eye.

God is
the eye of
the storm. The
center of God is perfect peace:
perfect calmness.
The eye of the storm is the center of the action;
where there is perfect stillness.
Everything around is in motion, yet the eye is not. He
wants us to enter into the calm place.
To bring our hearts into a calm place where He lives. When we
are able to see things from His
vantage, then a calmness will prevail. It is an unnatural calmness
only found in the center of
the eye: the center of His will. Not until we find the center of
His vision, will we be at
peace. When His vision and our vision meet, then
our eyes will meet
His eyes; and we will find that place
of perfect
peace.

Treasure

Your magnificence exceeds our ability to know You, O God.

But, yet You allow us to be found in You.

We are the treasure in Your bosom.

The treasure in your chest.

Your delight, reflecting the eye of Your glory.

We have become the am in the I.

Flowers From God's Nursery

Dream: I wake up passing God on the way to the Plant Nursery. I have a red wagon. He asks me if I have received any today. I say, "No."

Then he takes me into the nursery and fills my wagon up with flowers. Beautiful flowers.

Anointing

Often times we think anointing is given to a select group of believers who get a special gift from God. We think of it like a touch by a fairy's wand. They have told us that, "God called me."

We think that we need a burning bush or a Holy visitation to be anointed. This is not true. There is anointing waiting for all believers who seek Him, and are obedient to His words. To be anointed means that we have been set apart for a specific purpose. God has a purpose for each of us—a job in His Kingdom. Only, most of the time, we are the last ones to figure out what it is.

He tells us to love Him with all our heart, soul, and strength. When we first become believers we learn steps to love Him with our heart. Then, as we get our mind into the scriptures, we start to become changed. Our soul starts to love Him. Funny how our feet follow our heart and soul.

It is like when we walk from one green field to another. One field may be a field of oats and the other of rye grass. We walk from one area to the other. The first area is founded on oat seeds; these are the seeds of your own thinking—The way that you have been taught since you were small. You have built your ideas around these seeds of thought. An example might be, "Pull yourself up by your own bootstraps."

From this idea you put yourself through school and didn't depend on anybody for anything. But, as you walk into what God has for you, you come to a point where your thinking starts to change. The seeds change from oats to rye grass. The seeds of the scriptures start to grow in your mind. Perhaps you learn the verse that says, 'Trust in the Lord with all your heart. Do not depend on your own insight..." You start to change your ways of thinking about dependence on God. You have left the field of oats and entered into the field of the rye grass; you have began to walk into the anointing that God has already laid out for you. Then you can love Him with all your heart, soul and strength.

We see those with *an incredible anointing*. Actually, they are just further into the rye grass field. They have allowed their minds to be transformed with the seeds of the scriptures and their feet to walk in obedience further into the field that God has planned for them. We all have an incredible anointing because our God incredible God!

Become Empty

When we enter the Kingdom of God we become purified unto holiness. Then, we become anointed. To become anointed is to be set apart for a specific purpose and given a direction within that purpose. God is like a container that fills us up. We must come to Him with openness to be ready for Him to fill us up. We have to empty ourselves of what we are holding onto in order to have empty hands to do whatever He asks us to do. If our hands are already full of doing what we think that we are supposed to be doing, then we will not be available to do what He asks. He is the beaker that holds all we need for the service He wants to put us into. He will overflow to us. The Holy Spirit provides guidance. When He fills us, the anointing comes as part of the package. We are to become little cups, having been poured into by Him; we then are poured out to others. Our cup is filled with whatever the Lord has given us for a job within the Kingdom of God—whatever we hold in our hand to use for God. It is a cup, not a glass because it must have a 'handle' that is held by God.

When we learn to hear His voice and walk in obedience to it the oil of His joy flows into our cup. Then, there reaches a point when our cup is full to overflowing. If this cup, this anointing is near others, then it spills over to them. We walk in the reason that we were made. Our heart begins to actually sing. Others will notice. The anointing is meant to be our tithe to the Kingdom of God to be shared that God will be praised.

Genesis 8.11, Deuteronomy 14.23, Nehemiah 8, Esther 9.22, Job 33.26, Psalms 4.7, 28.7, 45.7, 71,104, 133, Isaiah 12.3, 56, 60, 61,65, Jeremiah 11.16. **Tanakh**.

Childlike Righteousness

The Dream: There is a porch with a clothesline is enclosed within a net. It looks like a fishnet, only it is positioned like a mosquito net around the porch.

Meditation: You can't show your own righteousness. You need to put up a clothesline on the porch to air out your righteousness.

For anyone self-righteous: With your mouth you say, but with your heart, you do.

True righteousness: When your heart demonstrates obedience to God. Buy righteousness from the little children. Ask them to sell it to you.

Interpretation of the Dream: This dream is instructing me to put my laundry on the front porch and let everyone see it. He will surround it with His *net*. He has made provision for my laundry.

The porch is the entryway between the road and the house. It is the place just before we go into the house. God wants us to deal with the laundry before we go into the house. We are to leave our old clothes on the doorstep when we enter into His presence.

He tells us to look at the children. Why? They show purity, innocence and speak from their heart. They do not try to hide things.

He says to buy it from the children. Have you ever tried to buy something from a child? They won't sell you anything because money does not mean anything to them. Their values are dependent on things that are dear to their heart, not their pocket book. They don't guard their identity because they don't care about it. They have not learned to be something that they are not.

God has given us everything we need for righteousness through His provision. We need to be careful not to sell it to others. His righteousness through us is free to others. Freely you have received, freely we are to give.

God is most interested in the condition of our heart. Often, we have been shamefully unfaithful to fulfill His word that has been given to us.

But, the Lord is merciful and forgiving, even though we have rebelled against Him by not obeying His voice. We need to give attention to His absolute truth. We ask for favor, not because of our own righteousness, but because of His mercy.

We should ask God to increase our faith; make us tender to His Spirit and teachable to the Spirit through the washing of His cleansing power. We do not seek our own righteousness, but to seek His kingdom and His righteousness to flow through us.

It is a faith venture. His grace is abundant and will fill the gap between our righteousness, our failure, and His righteousness. We are to offer the parts of our body as instruments of righteousness for His service. When we rely upon our own righteousness, it is like we have superseded God.

We cannot overpower the righteousness of God. We do not wrestle righteousness from God. It is a gift from faith in Him. This faith is put into our heart by injection of the Spirit who engraves His letter on our heart. This brings freedom in the Spirit because He is working inside us to fulfill His righteousness.

Joel 2:13, Proverbs 11:4-19 **Tanakh,** *II Corinthians 3:6-9, Galatians 3:21, Hebrews 7:2, James 3:18* **Christian New Testament,** *In the name of Allah, most gracious, most merciful. Surah 33.1* **Qur'aan**, *Mosiah 16.10-15* **Book of Mormon**.

Discipline and Discernment

From Proverbs, Ecclesiastes, and Job

Wisdom, knowledge and understanding go hand in hand with discipline. In order for our relationship with God to be two sided, there must be a response from us. God cannot come to our side of the table unless there is provision through grace and mercy. When we reach out to Him, then He speaks to us, we need to become obedient to His words to be able to walk into His presence. Holiness is acquired through walking into what He wants us to do. These are steps toward godly living.

We pass from one stage of glory to the next in our progression toward becoming what He wants us to become. As we give over areas of our lives to God, and fill them with His teaching and righteousness, then we move closer to Holiness. There gets to be *more of Him* and *less of us.*

Each time the inspiration from God comes to us, it calls for an action. Our obedience should be driven by love—His love for us and our gratefulness to Him. As He gives us words, we are to pay attention to what He says—listen closely. Then, when we walk, our steps will not be hampered, and when we run we will not stumble.

Once, when I was a teenager, we went to a Meeting at night. It was a small country Religious meeting in Leavenworth, Washington. It was way out in the country in the midst of huge timber trees. There was a youth building and a small church. They were across a bridge from each other. We played basketball in the youth center, and then walked to the Chapel for a service. This evening was very dark. It was the middle of winter. In this area, the snow gets very deep and the snow plow comes through on regular basis to clear the roads. This night we played later than usual, then had to race to the Chapel for the meeting. I was a good runner, so I thought I would out run every one. So, I took off running for all I was worth to cross that bridge to the Chapel building before others.

I did not plan on a huge ice chunk in the road. It had been left by a snow plow. I could not see it in the dark. I flew over that huge chunk of snow/ice combination and saw stars (that were not in the sky) for some time. Nobody even knew that I fell until they reached the Church.

It was too dark for them to see me fall. They came back and found me sprawled out in the road.

It is like this with God. We live in the dark. Without His light we cannot see. We certainly can't count on those nearby to help us because they can't see either. They won't know that we are not there until they reach the end and see that we did not make it.

The guidelines made by God are for our protection to keep us from falling over huge chunks in the road left by the snow plow.

Discernment

Discernment is not a separate spiritual gift. It is the ability to tell good from evil. When we discern something, it means that we can tell the difference between whatever it is coming from God or not from Him. Any child of God that has the Spirit, should have the spirit of discernment.

However, the closer we get to the mind of God, the easier it will be to tell the difference between the things that He has made and those that He has not. We will learn the character of God and recognize His handiwork. The ability to recognize what is 'not God' from what 'is of God' comes to life because you know the artist.

I have several paintings on my walls by famous artists. I am familiar with these paintings because I look at them every day and could easily tell if others were done by the same artist if I was shown another one and asked. When I am presented with something by someone and wonder if it is *of God*. I ask the Spirit of God to tell me the answer. I do not rely on my knowledge of Him. The Spirit of God will tell us if the enemy is at work, or if this work is from Him.

Remember—*Desire, determination and discipline—two out of three don't make you a winner.*

Over the Line

We won't stay because we won't pay.
When our relationship with the Lord stops being
convenient and moves to being inconvenient,
we have stepped over the line.

Running the Race

The Dream: *There is a mouse running in circles in the plant. It is a plant that was my mother's. She is in heaven. The mouse was like he was running a track. He was running just as fast as his little legs could carry him without stopping around and around.*

Interpretation of the dream: The plant is from my mother. Because my mother is in Heaven, the plant symbolizes, to me, the growth in the Kingdom of Heaven here on earth. The dirt is the earth. We live within earthen pots here on the earth. I am the mouse.

I am on track, even though I feel like I am running in circles, God has a plan and I can't see it because I am just looking at the bush, the dirt, and the pot. The growth of our religion (bush) now, the sin (dirt) in our lives, and trying to live a good life (running mouse) while entrapped in earthen vessels. I can't see God's ultimate purposes, only what He has put in front of me. He has me circling the growth on a track. I am wedged in there just right. In motion. He is sending me around the growth of the Kingdom.

Just like the mouse running in circles in the pot, I will have walls continually before me. These walls are to turn me, not stop progress. They won't stand in front of me unless I am facing the wrong direction. It's about following the plans He has for me and being on track.

Others may look at what I am doing and see no purpose. To them I look merely like I am running a race in vain. It looks like foolishness. But God has chosen the foolish in this world, to confound the wise.

God is a forever kind of a God. He wants things to go on and on. His love runs forever. His Holiness continues on and on. Redemption is unending. Might and power to us are forever. We run in His path because He has set our hearts free to be able to do it. He does not lead us like a trail leader. We do not walk behind Him, we walk beside Him keeping in step with Him.

When we walk with Him, He provides with inner strength just like having a steady supply of power bars. We are able to run so fast it seems like we are flying. And we are; we are in an elevated position with Him. Whenever we hold onto the hand of our Father, He brings us up to His spiritual level.

Sometimes we will not see the end because the purpose is not for us, but for others. Many times there is a great deal of preparation that goes into a specific work that God is doing. There are several steps and He must bring a lot of people together to achieve it. We may simply be a part of a bigger picture; a bigger work He is doing. When we do our part, then He can put the whole thing together. The vision waits until the appointed time, and then it happens at just the right time.

> "For the vision is yet for the appointed [future] time It hurries toward the goal [of fulfillment]; it will not fail. Even though it delays, wait [patiently] for it, Because it will certainly come; it will not delay. Habakkuk 2.3 ***Tanakh AMP***

Therefore, let us toss aside everything that weighs us down. We need to take off the weighs so that we can run faster. Only when we give him our burdens, can we have the endurance to run the race that He has for us. When we have put aside the cloud of our problems, then we can focus on what He has for us. We need to take out a pen and paper and start writing down what He wants us to do, pray for the grace to do it, and do it. Step out; move forward, walk into what He has already prepared for us.

Ezekiel 8.5, I Kings 19.20, Psalms 23, 58.7, 59.4, 77, 119, 147.15, Proverbs 4, 18, Song of Sol 1.4, Isaiah 40, **Tanakh,** *I Corinthians 9.24, Galatians 2, Philippians 2.16, Hebrews 12. Christian **New Testament.***

Dangling Conversation

Ambiguity and questioning: Seeking answers when we don't even know the questions. We just know something is not right about where we are. There is an uneasy feeling within our spirit. Something is missing, or not right. How do we amend that feeling?

Ask.

Get rid of the ambiguity. Question God. For He answers. He will provide The answer to us when we go to the place where we feel secure enough in the relationship to pop questions on the spur of the moment.

You know. You have those people that you can call up and continue conversation that you started yesterday. You don't need to tell the topic, because you both know it. Start, mid sentence, continue the conversation. Our relationship with God should be this way.

One of continual conversation in our spirit. We should be able to pick up the phone call Him and continue the conversation in the middle.

Then, not feel obligated to finish. Go ahead. Leave it dangling.

Transformation

The Spirits is the whisper in the wind on the other side.

The Voice of abundance.

Check this one out: What happens?

God talks to Him. His mind becomes God focused.

He turns to God. He changes. Transformation has happened.

Chapter 5
Meeting the Glory

Glory Pass

Be overrun with His love.

Sense Him coming like a runner up from behind.

Rather than trying to outrun, slow down; let Him encroach and overtake. Let Him pass.

For, when He gets in front, He shares a delivery from heaven; beautiful gifts.

We cannot openly receive while running away from Him.

Relax the stride long enough and allow Him to come around; encircle, and pass.

This is the glory pass.

Climb to Heights

The adventure is in climbing the mountain.
The wind is in our face. The glow from the reflection
of the sunrise on our face. Because He does talk, you know.
His whisper is like the wind. Climb to heights with Him.
To climb the face of a mountain, you need rope and sturdy
footholds. His position provides our footholds because
when we are His followers, His position becomes
ours by inheritance. He climbed the mountain
first and left the pegs in the rock for us
to use to hold onto. The ropes
are the word to us today.
Then there's grace
if
we slip,
the safety rope.
When the face opens,
that is the
eyes and
mouth.
The
face
of
God,
the cleft,
the place
where God's
face
is opened.
See, hear. Kiss
into the wind. That is where I live.
My wind kisses back. Be enthralled with
My love. Breathe, Inhale Me: My essence

Worldly Wisdom Melt Down

Worldly wisdom is like a mold used to make ice cubes. Everything is cool until things start to heat up. Then we have a tendency to have an emotional melt down. Wisdom from above comes with its own wall unit. AC/DC power source, making us a lot more even tempered.

Gun Powder in the Fire

The love

of God is amazing.

Throw

the gun powder into the fire

and watch the columns of flame.

Shock and awe. Go there at night.

Go to the flame. Be warmed and awed.

He is the one who sparks the flame.

When did I

forget?

I am

your anything.

When did you start remembering?

Don't forget. I remember.

I Am.

Song of Songs

Growing in Intimacy

There is a tree in the spiritual Kingdom that is alive. We need to become part of that tree to have life in our spirit. There is syrup, like maple syrup, that can be drawn off the tree. The syrup is the love of God that flows through the tree. The ability for the syrup to give life to the tree is through the Spirit of God. This tree does not have syrup, however, it has oil. The oil is the Spirit that flows through the tree out to the branches.

This is a special tree called the Tree of Life. It brings unity with God.   What makes the tree grow is when we are in unity with Him. It is a tree *nurtured* by our relationship because of His love for us. We are *plugged* into Him like the branches are plugged into a tree. We draw energy, or sap, from the root as it flows through the tree. The root is the love of God. He puts the branches wherever He wants on the tree.

When we put effort into spending time with Him, praying and listening to what He has to say, we will mature into His desire for us. whatever He wants us to be. We can become useful for others.

When we are attached to Him, then we begin to have a symbiotic relationship with Him. Just as the tree needs leaves, to draw sunlight and change it into energy, God needs us. The whole relationship is bathed in His love, like the sap of the tree.

We are His new growth and when we have been grafted into the original tree we become as pure as the root.

Song of Solomon, Chapter 1, **Tanakh**

Guardian of our Soul

Often, we care for others, but fail to care for our own heart. God has provided us a caretaker of our heart; Himself. We need to allow our heart to fall in love with Him; let Him care for us. He declares the things that flow from our heart are very special. They need to be guarded by someone who loves us. No one can guard our hearts like God.

When we entrust our heart to another above God, then it is like leaving a flock in the field without a shepherd to guard it. We can try to hide the sheep, but they are left unprotected. We can find companionship with others, but there is none that will guard our heart but God alone. He is the true shepherd of the soul.

Song of Solomon, Chapter 2.1-8, **Tanakh.**

Our Garden is Locked

When we refuse Him, He will turn away from us. When we lock the gate to our heart, He cannot come in. He comes only to gardens that are open to Him. Sometimes when He talks, we don't understand. We can go back to Him and ask Him for the *rest* of the message. Maybe it is a two part love message. We step out too soon without receiving the rest of the message. We need to return to Him for clarification when we don't understand what He is saying to us.

When our garden is open to Him, He will come often to visit us. He will trim the plants; give us direction. He wants to pasture His flock amidst the garden. He provides direction to His sheep through the pruning of the plants. He intertwines with us in a loving relationship and directs us. Through this He will direct believers. We may leave gifts for Him. They are the fragrance of our life as we live in devotion to His will. This is as a lily grown from a bulb. The bulb is like a light that He gives us. He may show us something and we walk into that light. This is fragrant to Him and He picks up on this. It is like He is the gardener and picks the flowers as He walks by. He picks and arranges them, then gives them to His lover—us. He arranges the things He is teaching us as bouquets when we turn them over to Him and He gives them back to us to adorn the table of His presence again.

We are all like a wall in the eyes of God until we open our hearts to Him to receive His love. We can only love Him with the love that He provides to us. He will trade our *wall* in for peace with Him. The walls are our responsibility. We built them—we must make them go away. He wants our garden to be adjacent to His without a wall between. He doesn't just want an open gate where He can come in occasionally. We each have our own vineyard and God wants to be our husband, to care for us. He wants us to remove the walls, sit in the garden and become

His companion listening for His voice. He wants to hear ours and be heard in our garden. Not simply as one yelling over a wall. Hurry.

Our garden is locked up and we have been given the key to unlock it. It is when we call out to Him, He will come to us and unlock us. We have springs that long to flow out of the garden to others, but they can't until the garden is unlocked.

Love unlocks the door. We have a rock garden within our walls. The Power of God is restrained when our garden is locked. We are His planting amidst the rocks, fed by His spring. We come to Him and receive the fruits of the Spirit of God. Then we learn to listen to His voice for direction. We continue to press in to learn to love Him. He shows us His face; we see Him as He really is. Then we see the direction for the Kingdom of God and where we belong in it. He provides the power *rock* of the Spirit within our lives out poured *water* within the gifts. We are a rock garden when we are mature in the gifts He has given us. Gifts *plants* with direction *springs that flow* and power *rocks*.

The fruit comes from the rock garden. When the tree is planted by the streams of God, the fruit will be full of seeds just like a pomegranate. The stream flows from the love of God to feed the tree—from the highest place in heaven. It is from a well of fresh water that will continue to flow forever.

*Song of Solomon, 2, **Tanakh***.

Intimacy of the Secret Place

When we come to Him, seeking His love, He will sustain that intimacy. It is not like a relationship with a boyfriend that may falter when one of you looses interest. No, God says that He will maintain interest in us and put in our hearts to maintain interest in Him. He takes responsibility for maintaining both sides of the relationship when the Spirit dwells within. His fruit continues to supply us with what is needed to make the relationship eternal. He sustains and refreshes. We become lovesick. And, if we press into the relationship with Him, we will stay lovesick. Nothing will help—we are swooned with His love.

He puts His left hand under our head, and embraces us with His right hand. He puts, not only just one hand on us, but both.

When God puts His hand on something, it stays. We are so valuable—He is holding us with both of His hands. Like a valued blanket held in the hands of a two year old. He values us. Like the ashes of one's lost mother. He holds us with two hands so we can't fall, can't leave, and can't break loose. He holds us in His hands of love. He is lovesick for us.

His love is so strong, that if it is aroused, He becomes as a jealous lover. He comes with everything that is a lover and God at the same time. When He is called upon as Counselor, He will become Counselor. When He is called upon as *intimate friend* this is a new ball game. His feelings of intimacy for us are aroused. When we are ready for this type of relationship, we can be sure, He will accommodate. He will come quickly because He has been waiting since eternity past for us. We have only been here for a short time, but He has been planning for this love relationship for a long time.

Did you know God loves our feet? It is our feet that enable us to move. The movement of us here on earth spreads His words to others. He likes to watch our walk. He guides us with His eye upon us every second. The unfolding of our life is like a painting in the hand of an artist. God is the artist and we are the canvass. He loves everything about us. He is captivated by us.

He climbs mountains and leaps hills like a gazelle to come to us. The only thing that has stopped Him before was the wall that we built to keep Him out. He will not come through walls, no matter what they are built of. He only comes through open doors. hey are opened from the inside out. We have to open our heart to Him. Many times we wall off our heart to God. We try to protect it from pain, but in protecting it from pain—we keep it from the place where God can love us freely.

We leave Him to look through the windows and peep through the lattice to see how we are doing. Even though He planted the garden, we have closed off the wall to Him and refuse to allow Him to tend it. He created our hearts and He has given us the ability to love Him and others. Yet, we close off our heart to Him. We build a wall to keep Him out of areas that we consider *private.* He wants to be invited into those private gardens. Those private gardens of our hearts, the place where the most cherished flowers are. These are the areas of our most valued thoughts.

When we ask Him to come to our *garden* He will come. He will go through the door. The door is the provision of grace and mercy.

Many times we want God to be flesh. He isn't. Wisdom through the Spirit of God instructs as a brother. We can freely share all with the Spirit—He will listen. When we ask for the Love of God to come into our heart, He will come with all of His zeal. He will seal our heart for ever. He will ignite the flame of our heart toward Him in a way we could never do. Nothing can quench His love in our heart.

There is another door, just like a second door that comes from the foyer to the kitchen that must be opened. This door is opened by walking toward the love of God. We are drawn by His love to this room. We must learn to listen to His voice and walk toward it. The room is dark and He provides the way to the light switch, but we must listen to His directions to get to the switch. We need to learn how to switch from human love and emotions to *God love and fruits of the Spirit.*

Song of Solomon, Chapter 3, ***Tanakh.***

Garden of Expectation

It is good. It is right for Him to give assignment to those He loves.
We need to live in the garden of His expectation.

Wanderers

We have wandered in our day dreams clogging our mind so
God can't speak to us at night.

Great Faithfulness

Great is Your faithfulness.
For when Yours is great, ours does not really need to be.

Sandwiched Between

When God turns the light on, we will begin to see things His way. We will go from sleep, to awake. There is a certain level that the noise reaches when we wake up. We hear. We don't see first, we hear, then we see. We are sandwiched between now and later and listen, learn to listen. Get yourself a ride to between now and later, here and eternity, the place where His voice meets His power.

The lighted place where we see things, as He does. Over, under, around, and through. Where's thou? Down the middle. In the cleft.

God Reveals Himself

The love which we love God is that which He has told us about. We know nothing of God unless He tells us of Himself. So, we all love Him differently because He reveals Himself differently to each of us. No doubt, He is dazzling to all. He is wondrous and amazing. None compares with Him as He reaches out to our heart. He gives only the best gifts. He shows us only the purest form love. Each time He reveals more of Himself, we melt. Whether we are a new believer or a mature one, His love comes to make our heart throb. His voice drips of His admiration for us each time He speaks. His voice displayed through the Spirit is upheld by the power of His Name. He is true to every word. He is not built by us, but continues to build us day by day. He desires to be our beloved and our friend, both. Let Him.

*Song of Solomon, 2.14, **Tanakh**.*

Walking Along the Fence

Sometimes when we are put into the field, we are scared of it.
We run along the fence peering over at our old life.
There is a trail that leads to the next gate, only
a field. So, we follow our friends and our
momma. They only lead us back
to the barn. They take us out
of the field God has for us.
They bring us to their desires,
not God's. If their desires are for God, the Lord
in Heaven, they are good, but they lead us to a different side
of the pasture than the one we need to go to. So, we inch along the
fence trying to look nonchalant, like we know where we are going.
But the fence only leads us in circles. We end up around the promise
land, but never enter in. We watch the good things from a distance.
Others get, we don't. We have joined forces with the *have nots.*
What to do?
Take a step into the field—the field that God has called us to.
It is the one He has put us into. We need to step toward
His promises and follow His word. It always leads
to Him. He is just over the rise. A shepherd
calls to his flock and they know
his voice. Why would he call
and not expect for
them to come?

Training

There is a charm school in the Kingdom of God. He provided us a school—a training program to learn about Him. In this school we learn to walk with poise. Like those girls with a book on their head. We need to put His book on our head—the Scriptures. When we complete God's charm school His love will flow through us using the gifts He provides.

He looks on us with all of the pride of a father when his daughter walks the breezeway as a model. He is charmed by us when we walk in His love. He is happy because He knows that our tree will always produce fruit in and out of season. At any time He can send someone to us and we will drop fruit on them. They can pick from our branches and receive whatever He wants for them to have. We have become fruitful. When we walk, with every hip movement there is fruit dropping everywhere. He loves it. We are like a speed boat with a rooster tail. He likes to watch the tail and the wake and each wave afterwards. Many lives are changed by one who is walking in the gifts, the presence and the joy of the Lord.

God's desire is only for our best—He wants to send us into specific areas that have not become part of His kingdom. They are villages yet. He has called us to help others to grow into what God wants them to become. He will tell us which stage others are in with their growth. He will help us to provide what they need to help them get to where they need to go. Wherever they are, they need to start seeking His love. Infuse their situation with His love. God has a fruit basket waiting for each of us. We must open the door of our heart to Him.

*Song of Solomon, Chapter 4, **Tanakh**.*

Garden Visit

I passed and He sang to me.

I stopped and He wrote to me.

I visited His garden and He talked to me.

Dreams

This love relationship with God is sticky. Like honey. We will become His honey and He will be ours. Only, when He comes to eat our honey that grows in our trees—He not only eats the honey, but the comb. He is zealous for our love. He wants to be as our lover. To spend endless time, continual dining on His presence. He will feed us with whatever we nee—Help us to understand Him and be to us a personal God. When we want snacks in the middle of the night, He will give us warm milk *dreams.* When we are ready for full course meals, He will come *to bring understanding of Scriptures.* He calls us to imbibe deeply as a lover. To deepen our love for Him as much as possible.

When we become believers, we are made new. He gives us a new heart that longs to seek His heart. Just as God never sleep—our new spiritual awakening is such that our heart will seek His heart day and night. At night, He will come knocking on our door; on the door of our heart. It is a time when our flesh is asleep and our will lies dormant. Our spirit is open to Him.

He slices between our soul, flesh and spirit to give us messages of His love—love notes from God. He desires us to be open with Him. Why can't we open up to Him? We are selfish. We guard our thoughts and our hearts. We build walls around them and fortify them with our disobedience.

He comes out of His house in heaven at night to speak with us. He is drenched with dew. But we are afraid that it is not Him speaking to us. Our fear keeps us from extending our hands to Him. We are afraid that it is our own mind talking to us, and not Him. We are afraid that we have been found not clean in His sight. So, we cut Him off. We refuse to believe that He leaves His security of heaven, come down to earth and speak personal messages to us. We don't go along with His voice at night. Maybe we are too lazy to get up and write the dream down. It is a love note. Like the ones a young love puts in a lunch box to be opened later. They are riddles.

He wraps them as gifts to be opened later in His presence. Just like at

Christmas. When we give a gift, we wrap it up. It is the most fun if we open it in the presence of the giver. The dreams are to be opened up in the presence of the giver; God.

God is extending His hand through the window He has opened in our world. When He reaches out His hand to us, our feelings are aroused for Him. When we listen to Him—we will hear of His love for us. We can't but love Him back. The dream is a window, it is not God Himself. We will become disappointed if we think we will find God there. It is His message, not Him. Our heart should throb and reach out to Him as He speaks to us. We need to open the package that He has dropped on our doorstep. We cannot go after the postman. He has already left.

Others will think we are crazy to pursue someone that we cannot see. To seek someone that we will never be able to physically love here on earth. We can never grab hold of God because He is Spirit. To others we are pursuing spirits. Satan will try to make us look silly. And to the world, we will look silly. He can take our stuff, but God owns our heart. He can't touch that. Once it is put into the hand of God, no one can touch it.

The love of God is surprising. It does not have any relationship with religion. We seem to stumble around in this world until we start to see that all of things that are important are related to His love for us. Often, we study scriptures, pray and talk to God not understanding His love.

We need to press in for His love. Stand on our tip toes and look over the fence toward His Kingdom. He gives us strands of knowledge in visions, dreams and His word to us. When we catch as many of these strands as possible, we will become enthralled to learn of His true love. Because, when He sees us peeking over the fence at Him, guess what? He will jump over your fence to join our party. Before we are aware of what hit us, He sets our soul free to love Him. He helps us to enter into His royal procession to the throne of God.

*Song of Solomon, Chapter 3-6, **Tanakh.***

God's Clippers

The Lord wants to be our vine dresser—our husband. He wants to come to us and gather fruit from us, press it and make wine to be served to others. He selects the fruit that is ripe and develops it into a ministry that will serve others. God has given us all things freely to enjoy. He wants us to learn of Him from the ministry that He has given us as we listen to His voice for direction.

When God shows up with His love, He brings His clippers. We are like a tree that has been allowed to grow year after year without direction. He wants to give us direction; He provides the pruning to our tree. His voice will provide the direction—the pruning that is needed in our lives. His voice is sweet, calm and low. It sounds like a turtledove to our ears. He coos us like a mother with a baby. He knows the season and He knows just how much potential our tree has for bearing fruit. He will trim off any of the things that will keep us from bearing fruit. The fruits of righteousness; love, joy, peace, patience, patience, kindness, goodness, faithfulness, gentleness, self control. He helps to rid the things of the flesh which keep the tree from growing healthy and producing a good crop.

When our tree is pruned, given direction, it will bear fruit. The fragrance of the fruit will be given to others. It will have seeds from the original tree; the tree of life, which is the love of God.

Then, God continues to lead us. He doesn't stop there with just producing a fine crop from our trees. He wants us to continue to press into His love and companionship. He puts us back into the cleft of the rock and passes over us again and again. He takes us to His secret garden—His secret place. He can now trust us because we have allowed ourselves to be pruned *directed* by Him and have born fragrant fruit. Then, He will let us not only hear Him, but see Him. We will connect the voice with a face. He comes to each of us differently, but our response is the same. He has made us glasses to see Him. The glasses have to be put on. They are prescription specially prepared for each of us. It is the anointing that He has given us. When we move toward Him and listen to His voice, our mind begins to be changed into His likeness. The more we are changed and the more we come to recognize His voice, we will *see* Him when He shows up. He will show Himself to us. He trusts us as a faithful servant because we have been found faithful with hearing and obeying, now He will allow us to see.

Song of Solomon, Chapters 6-8, ***Tanakh****.*

Sure Footed Decisiveness

Indecision,

indecisiveness

instinctively insists on stalling

until they get their own way.

Thorough bread horses run the race with decisiveness

and sure footedness from the gate to the ribbon.

We need to.

Worship Image

Be careful, She's gone now. She worshiped the marriage, not the person. Sometimes we worship an image of what we think the relationship with God should be, instead of Him.

Jonah

Jonah got out of the belly of the whale—the bonds of death—the agony of defeat, a desperate situation, by asking the only one who could talk to whales... and they obey. Is your whale too big? Stop asking it. Ask Him who controls it. It's not really about control.

It's about obedience. The whale is obedient to his maker. God doesn't want our head. He Is. He wants us to see His mind through the eyes that He has put in our heart. But we are like kittens born without seeing. Our eyes need to be opened to see spiritual things.

Fragrance

When we come to His table, we smell good to Him. Our presence is like sweet perfume to Him. He wants us to get close enough to smell us. Get close. Us to Him. Scoot near to His chair, not only the table. He wants us to lean on His breast; to hear His heart beat. Lay our ear on His chest.

He sees the potential in us that is stored up. We are like a beautiful cherry tree full of blossoms ready to bloom. He can hardly wait to see the cherries come. They provide food for others. He thinks we are absolutely beautiful. There is not one part of us that He doesn't like.

Then, as we get close to Him, we discover that we too, will delight in Him. We will see the beauty in His face. He is handsome as a new lover is to the other. He wants us to linger with Him, to talk with Him and listen to Him talk. He wants to have heart to heart conversation with us. To just lie back on the couch and hang out. He will be our counselor if we ask Him whenever we need one. But, mostly, like a new lover, He wants to be our intimate friend. There is fragrance and beauty when our relationship is through the love of the Spirit. The robe of mercy and grace covers sin. There is nothing but beauty, freedom from the decay of sin when we cling to His provision for forgiveness of sin. We become both beautiful and fragrant in His eyes. We are one of a kind in His eyes; the most beautiful flower in the garden. He sees us as a beautiful rose amidst the thorns in the garden. He is not intimidated by the thorns, He knows them well. He knows about how we become wounded by others. We have scratches and scars from living here on the earth, but yet, He overlooks all of these to smell our perfume and gaze at our beauty.

When we find the heart of God, it will be like finding an apple tree in a forest. We will have thought we were lost and hungry, but He gives refreshment and food. It will be food for our soul and spirit. He provides shade for us—a retreat from all else. We can find rest for our soul, when we come to His tree. He wants us not to run by, but to sit down for a while and rest under the shade of His presence. Allow His presence to pass over us like it did over Moses when He placed him in the crevice of the rock and placed His hand over him.

Through the provision of the Spirit, He turns His presence into one of delighting daily. He wants us to take delight in Him. He gives us one sign after another of His love. Everything He gives us is a sign of His love. When we come close to His heart, we will recognize it. He draws us with loving kindness. Nothing else. When we ask, He opens our eyes to see it.

Song of Solomon, **Tanakh.**

Ideas Drive Momentum

Truth

 decapitates

the thought

process from the

flesh we live in.

Ideas drive momentum.

If Satan can control our ideas,

he can steer our body.

His ideas drive

our flesh.

Be careful: When you feel the

first tug toward something in your flesh.

Strobe Light Walk

Sometimes it doesn't look like we're moving
because we are in a room with strobe light.
We only see with glimpses of light that
God provides for only a few seconds. Faith walk.

Copy the Answer

We need to take note of what He tells us.
Copy the answer. His Words are the answer,
so when we realize which aspect of His character
we need to emulate, then copy.

Spirit of Might Explosion

Goodness and Praise flow from the same source.
The Only True God! The living God.
He is good. His Mercy endures!
How we praise Him!
We lift Him up!
How, He Praises us.
Then, His goodness is
pressed into our lives.
Goodness and praise;
Characteristics of God
given to His people through
endearment. Provision through
the Spirit of Might. His vision, our
vision. His power Explosion into action.

The Parade

The couch of Go—His counseling couch is a traveling couch. Like the sedan chair of King Solomon, it is made from the timber of Lebanon. It is from the strength of mighty trees that we are lifted. It has posts of silver and a back of gold with a seat of purple fabric. Our seat in the parade toward the kingdom of God is one of a royal procession sitting next to the King. He has unlimited access to all of the riches in the world. He provided the interior of the coach to meet our specifications. He has gone ahead and lovingly fitted it to our needs and desires. It is like a coach being drawn by His power and love as the horses. He wants to sit next to us and whisper into our ear. He provides angelic presence to confirm His presence and word. It is like we are in a parade. Not merely in a parade that we don't know where it is going. The head of the parade is sitting next to us telling us each move of the procession toward the Kingdom of God.

This isn't a parade like a festive parade—it is a parade like one that welcomes an army home from battle. He wants us to become expert wielders of the sword—the scriptures, against the enemy. He desires us to win every battle against our enemies using the sword of the scriptures and the Spirit of Gos. He trains us to become expert swordsmen in His company. We are to march with Him as our leader. The sword is our guard against the terrors of night.

The parade goes toward the place where the crowning happens. Our Lord wants to crown us in His spiritual kingdom. When we climb aboard the coach, listen to Him and start down the center of the road that He has chosen for us, it leads to our crowning. When we pick up our crown, we begin to walk into the spiritual realm of the kingdom of God. We join the procession—the parade. We let Him teach and instruct us and we walk into His voice. To God, our Lord, when we do this—it is like a wedding day. There is unity between two families because there has been a marriage. There has been a marriage of the scriptures to the power of God by our obedience to His voice. It gives birth to His power being able to be activated here on earth. He has someone who will listen to Him, seek direction and follow Him for the right reason, because of His love.

Song of Solomon, **Tanakh.**

Wedding

It is the start of a love relationship, a joining on earth and in heaven. The wedding is consummated with a crown, like a tiara given to a bride. A spiritual gift is given, and it can be used for God's purposes. The individual is open to His direction using His tools for His kingdom. Ole! A banner day. Just like a wedding festival, there has been a joining of two. Us to God. He has become our husband and we have assumed the position as one of His plants that need care. We have put ourselves under His care, His pruning, etc. He has entered our garden.

As long as we are on the earth, there will be a veil between the eyes of God and our eyes. We can only see partially what God has for us. It is like looking at someone wearing reflective sunglasses. We cannot see His eyes, but reflect them. We see His crown—His royalty. We know that He has come down to our world for us

When God looks at us through the eyes of Mercy and Grace, He sees us as pure without blemish. We are like a bride to Him. He wants to swoop down and gather us up, just like a groom carries his new bride over the threshold. He wants to take us on a journey with Him to His place. He sees us as in need of being rescued from lions and leopards. He wants to be our knight in shining armor and carry us away on His white horse. When we turn our heart to Him, we make His heart pound. But, as we are not His bride, only betrothed, there remains purity in the relationship. It is a very intense love, however. For with one single glance of our eyes toward Him, His heart skips beats and He can't control His emotions toward us. When God's love is turned on, His loving kindness is directed and He can't control Himself. His zeal overtakes Himself. He loves us too much.

God loves to hear us talk to Him. He likes to hear our voice. Each time He hears our voice, it is like we have been gone on a trip and He can't wait to hear it again.

Song of Solomon, Chapter 4, **Tanakh.**

Leap of Faith

Puddle jumping children take risks.
How far it is too far? How close
is not far enough?
To be free
to step
from
towards
To take
a leap
of faith
over the puddles
in your life and know
for sure He will keep you from falling.
But, why do children leap puddles after the rain?
A boundary has been set and you want to know
if you can keep on the right side of the line.
It's risky and you may not make it.
Adventure and danger.
Ability to perform meets
desire within boundaries.
Sounds like a spiritual walk.
You can tell those who look for puddles.
Their lives are exciting, but their shoes are a bit muddy

Sheri Hauser is from Seattle, Washington and attended Bible College right out of high school in Cannon Beach, Oregon. A few years after that she registered to go to school and become a nurse. She worked her way up the field of nursing to become a Cardiac ICU Nurse and stayed at a hospital in Las Vegas for 15 years. In 2005, she received the baptism of the Holy Spirit and began having vivid dreams and visions which sparked her writing prompting the release of a series of books related to the topic of hearing the voice of God. The interest in writing grew into an interest in publishing and she attended University of Las Vegas launching into the educational aspects needed to become a book publisher. Glorybound Publishing was started in 2005 and has continued to explode publishing over 700 books by 2026.

Sheri Hauser has continued to expand her knowledge base as the years have clicked by earning credentials as a Sound Engineer (for opening the book recording studio) and Social Media Marketing. The Social Media Marketing has pushed book marketing into the modern age. When combined with being a webmaster, authors have an advantage publishing their books with Glorybound Publishing. In 2026 Glorybound Publishing has 18 book marketing websites and a website dedicated to in depth training for modern-day book marketing.

Miracule's was the first book...and indeed...it did cause an explosion of a miracle. Amen.

POETRY INDEX

sheri@gloryboundpublishing.com
www.gloryboundpublishing.com